Joseph Nicolar

The Life and Traditions of the Red Men

Joseph Nicolar

The Life and Traditions of the Red Men

ISBN/EAN: 9783337055851

Printed in Europe, USA, Canada, Australia, Japan

Cover: Foto ©ninafisch / pixelio.de

More available books at **www.hansebooks.com**

Joseph Nicolar

THE

LIFE AND TRADITIONS

OF

THE RED MAN

BY

JOSEPH NICOLAR

Old Town, Maine

Bangor, Maine
C. H. Glass & Co., Printers
1893

PREFACE.

IN offering this work which will give the public the full account of all the pure traditions which have been handed down from the beginning of the red man's world to the present time, I deem it proper to state that there have been no historical works of the white man, nor any other written history from any source quoted.

All prophesies, theories and ideas of the educated and intelligent of all races have been laid aside; no supposition nor presumption of any class entertained, because it is intended to show only the simple and natural state of the life, habits and ways as they existed among the pure, innocent and simple people whose traditions are here written.

Simple as one would imagine them to be, yet some prophesies of theirs when given a full account of, will be very interesting, especially when it is shown that none of the studies nor the researches of the white man have ever penetrated—thereby dwelt upon them. But still remains with him as hidden things.

Nevertheless, a close observer cannot fail to see that some of their prophesies are very significant and important, not only to the red man himself, but nations of all other races as well.

And this is not all! Because when his ways and habits are learned it will be found that they are so peculiar it has spread the veil over the eyes and minds of the learned of these modern dates, and have caused many to enquire, "Where did the red man come from?"

This is the question we intend to answer! We intend also, to remove the fear, that the life of the red man will pass away unwritten, and this is written because there is an abundance of evidence showing that there is a general desire among the people that some one ought to write it now if ever.

In this undertaking I wish to say to the public, that I am one of the descendants of the remnants of that once numerous and most powerful race; and my life having been spent in the researches of my people's past life, beginning in my early boyhood days to the present time I can say that, by the grace of nature I have been crowned with a success.

Only one thing is lacking; and that is the proper education to do such work, and one who reads this will be fully convinced when he sees that I was never educated to that degree as to be able to excite the feelings of the people and make them pronounce me as a brilliant and popular writer. However, I have undertaken the work and have done it in my own way; have given the full account of all the traditions as I have gathered them from my people.

After forty years of search and study I am satisfied that no more can be found, as the old traditional story tellers have all gone to the happy hunting ground.

Klose-kur-beh, "The Man From Nothing," was

claimed by all the children of the red man, to be the first person who came upon the earth. And he was their teacher! He taught them how they must live, and told them about the spiritual power, how it was in every living thing, and it was the same power that has sent him to prepare the way on earth for the generations to come; and to subdue all obstacles which are against the nature of mankind; and to reduce the earth to such a state as to become a happy land for the people.

The works of Klose-kur-beh were wonderful—traditions extend to the time of his presence among them, and his works and teaching, during his stay with his children, as he called all the people, will be fully written in this work. His coming into the world the instructions and power given him by the Great Spirit will be fully shown and explained. Also how great the love and reverence bestowed upon him by the people for his good works.

In reading the works, it can clearly be seen that this Klose-kur-beh was at the creation.

His claims to that effect were not only by his words, but also by his most wonderful works as will be shown in the following pages of this book.

JOSEPH NICOLAR.

OLD TOWN, MAINE, 1893.

CHAPTER I.

KLOSE–KUR–BEH, "The Man from Nothing," first called the minds of the "Red Children" to his coming into the world when the world contained no other man, in flesh, but himself. When he opened his eyes lying on his back in the dust, his head toward the rising of the sun and his feet toward the setting of the sun, the right hand pointing to the north and his left hand to the south. Having no strength to move any part of his body, yet the brightness of the day revealed to him all the glories of the whole world; the sun was at its highest, standing still, and beside it was the moon without motion and the stars were in their fixed places, while the firmament was in its beautiful blue. While yet his eyes were held fast in their sockets, he saw all that the world contained. Besides what the region of the air revealed to him, he saw the land, the sea, mountains, lakes, rivers, and the motion of the waters, and in it he saw the fishes. On the land were the animals and beasts, and in the air the birds. In the direction of the rising sun he saw the night approaching.

While the body clung to the dust he was without mind, and the flesh without feeling. At that moment the heavens were lit up, with all kinds of bright colors most beautiful, each color stood by itself, and in another moment every color shot a streak into the other, and soon all the colors intermingled, forming a beautiful brightness in the center of the heavens over the front of his face. Nearer and nearer came the brightness toward his body until it got almost to a touching distance, and a feeling came into his flesh, he felt the warmth of the approaching brightness, and he fell into a deep sleep. The wind of the heavens fanned his brow, and the sense of seeing returned unto him, but he saw not the brightness he beheld before, but instead of the brightness, a person like unto himself, standing at his right hand, and the person's face was toward the rising of the sun. In silence he raised his right hand, in the direction of the rising sun, passed it from thence to the setting of the sun, and immediately a streak of lightning followed the motion of his hand from one side of the earth to the other. Again he raised his right hand to the south, passing it to the north, and immediately another streak of lightning followed the motion of his hand. Immediately after the passing of the lightning over his body, a sense of thought came unto him. The first thought that came unto him was, that he believed the person was able to bring strength unto him, and the "Great Being" answered his thought saying these words: "Thou doest well believing in me, I am the head of all that thou beholdest, and as thou believest, arise from thy bed of dust, and stand on thy feet, let the dust be under thy feet, and as thou believest, thou shalt have

strength to walk." Immediately strength came unto
him, and he arose to his feet, and stood beside the
"Great Being".

After this the "Great Being" moved and turned half
around towards his right hand, facing the sun. Lifting
both hands and looking up he said : "Go thy way !" and
immediately the whole heavens obeyed. The sun,
moon and all the stars moved towards the setting
of the sun. The night coming slowly toward their
standing, when the Great Being sending up his voice,
saying : "Let us make man in our own image," and
immediately dropped his two hands and cast his eyes
upon the land and moved half way around again toward
his right hand, facing the setting of the sun, and
passed his right hand from the north to the south. The
lightning followed the motion of his hand, from the
north to the south, and again passing his hand from
the setting of the sun to the rising of the sun, immediately the lightning followed the motion of his right
hand, from the setting of the sun to the rising of the
sun, and when the lightning came upon the night
which was approaching it disappeared ; the darkness
of the night hid from them, what was beyond the night.

Immediately the dust of the land began to shake
and to heave, in the form of a cross, where the motion
had been made. And there was an image of a man
lay on the ground.—his head toward the north, and
his feet toward the south—his right hand pointing to
the setting of the sun, and his left hand toward the
rising of the sun, his face lay towards the blue skies
over their heads, and his face was white with the pale-

ness, because life was not yet in him; Klose-Kur-beh said, "and immediately the Great Being said unto me, 'Turn thy face to the setting of the sun,' and I obeyed him; and again the Great Being spoke unto me, saying 'I will not suffer thee to see this man arise to his feet like yourself therefore, go thy way, toward thy right hand and seek thy companions! I will be thy teacher and you will be their teacher;' and I obeyed his command."

Turning toward my right hand and facing the north. Behold! there was a high mountain seven rainbows high. To this I went, and up the mountain I walked; seven times my strength left me, and seven times the wind of the heavens fanned my brow, each time giving me strength to go on my way. Seven times I reached out my hand unto the seven rainbows and lifted myself on my feet, so that I was able to walk to the top of the mountain, and immediately a cloud of the heavens lowered, and lifted me from the top of the mountain, carrying me toward the rising of the sun, toward where the night was coming, and unto the night the clouds carried me, and unto the darkness I was carried and in the midst of the darkness a voice spoke unto me, saying, "even in the darkness I will be with thee." These words brought light into the clouds so that the clouds which carried me was like a ball of fire, and the ball of fire gave us light while passing the darkness of the night, and when the darkness of the night passed toward the setting of the sun, the light of the day came from the rising of the sun.—And the clouds turned white and the brightness of fire was not there. And the wind from the setting of the sun came upon the clouds, and shook the clouds so it began to break in pieces until all was scattered, leaving only a small mist which held me, which soon left me standing on my feet on the top of a high mountain, my face was toward the rising of the sun, and at this moment a voice spoke unto me, saying, "Turn again thy face to thy right hand, and thy face be toward the noon sun—this is South,—and thy back is toward the cold hand—this is North,—thy right hand now point to the setting of the sun,—this is West,—and thy left hand point to the rising of the sun,—this is East.   From the East and from the West, from the North and from the South, I will send the wind, to let you know that even the wind will obey me, and now I will command the sun to arise.   Go thy way toward the sun, and when the sun sets and night comes, there rest.   On the morrow arise with the sun, and go towards it until it sets.   Seventy times seven, shalt thou arise, with the sun, and walk towards it until it sets.   Seventy times seven nights will I visit thee, and teach thee thy duties.   At the end of thy journey there abide, and thy companion will come unto thee."   Immediately the sun arose and I started on my journey.

Thus by the command of the "Great Being," Klose-kur-beh started on his journey to find his companions.

The writer will now narrate in the following pages, a full account of all the original traditions, in a simple way and manner, so that even the small children will readily understand them.   .

The name of Klose-kur-beh was given to this wonderful being, after the people came and learned his teachings, and learned how he came into existence.

This name, or the word, Klose-kur-beh needs much explanation, since it has been the case in all languages that some of the old words have been changed, very often corrupting the word into something else, or changing its meaning. For instance, the word Klose-ki, in the old Indian language meant *simple* or *nothing*.

"Klose-ki-ner-quatt," is the word for *simple appearance*; and "Klose-kur-beh" means, the *man from nothing*.

But since there has been such a vast change in the Indian dialect, in later years, the word "Klose-kur-beh" is now understood, to mean a man of falsehood, or more vulgarly, a liar.

Should some of the Indian children read this work, they must bear in mind, that this word, "Klose-kur-beh" was not intended to be used as the word *liar*, as it will readily be seen that the original Indian phraseology remedies this corruption. Hence the word Klose-hur-beh must be allowed to rest on the original meaning.

After giving the account of the journey of Klose-kur-beh, in his own words, the writer will now use the words of the traditional story tellers.

So important was the duty which devolved upon them, that they were not only careful in all their tellings, but were watchful as well. They resorted to all sorts of penetrating efforts to learn and gather all that could be found for the benefit of their people, and after all that was done there still lies a veil over the period during the seventy times seven days, in which,

Klose-kur-beh travelled, because there was no mention made by him, whether he was fed and clothed during this journey or not. Therefore this part remains a mystery to this day. If Klose-kur-beh made mention of it, the story tellers did not. At a later period, the opinion of all the people agree that Klose-kur-beh did not reveal that part to them, and the people came to the conclusion that there was nothing said about it by Klose-kur-beh. It was clear to the minds of the people that Klose-kur-beh made particular mention of the seventy times seven nights of rest and of the visit of the "Great Being." In each of the visits seven words passed between them until the last seven days. In these last seven days Klose-kur-beh was fed and clothed, and shown how to obtain food, and with what to clothe himself. In all these days no seasons were mentioned until the last seven days came.

None of the traditions, located the country wherein all these things took place, but it was agreed by all interested in later years, that it was on the eastern part of the Red man's World : So much of this belief remained as a settled fact, that the people began to look for the appearance of other people in that direction, which proved to them afterwards that their belief was a true one. Another evidence which strongly points to indicate the true location, is that the last seven days Klose-kur-beh comes to an open sea every morning while going in the direction of the rising of the sun.

The teaching of the Great Being to Klose-kur-beh was very lengthy. In the first seven nights the Great

Being made known to Klose-kur-beh that the world was all spiritual, that there was a *living* spirit in all things, and the spirit of all things has power over all, and as the spirit of all things center in Him, he was the Great Spirit, by His will, all things move, all power comes from Him; and he—"Klose-kur-beh" must teach the people that there is but one Great Spirit.

When Klose-kur-beh was teaching his people, he points out to them where the Great Spirit was:—in the sun—moon—stars—clouds of heaven—mountains, and even in the trees of the earth. After the teaching of Klose-kur-beh had been sown and had taken root, then all the Red men could be seen to make signs of reverance and worship, when any of these things met their gaze.

The religious teaching of Klose-kur-beh did not bear much fruit until after he had shown the people, the power given him by the Great Spirit. Klose-kur-beh must have seen the unfruitfulness of his teaching, because he began to say to them, that he would very soon begin to show them by his works, that every word he said to them was true. After he had accomplished all he was charged to do by the Great Spirit, then the people declared his teaching to be all true.

Three things of Klose-kur-beh's teaching are held more sacred than all others.

The first was the power of the Great Spirit.

Second, the land the Great Spirit gave them they must never leave, and the third, they must never forget their first mother, but must always show the love they have for her, and all work must cease during the observances of her honor.

Before going further with the work, it is necessary to give an account of Klose-kur-beh meeting his companions, and after giving fully of all the particulars of that eventful period, I shall enter again into the account of his teaching.

After the seventy times seven nights had passed, when the sun was highest, a person came unto Klose-kur-beh from the rising of the sun; the one who came was a woman and she was bowed down with old age. She began to speak unto Klose-kur-beh, saying: "Noo-sus—my grandson," to which Klose-kur-beh answered: "Ka-goos Nok-a-mi,—what is it my grandmother?" and Nok-a-mi said: "I have come to stay and I will be useful in preparing food for you. I have no other place to go; I know of no other person but you; I am bowed down with old age; yet I came into existance this very noon-day sun, and owe my existance to the dew of the rock, and as the noon-day sun shineth hot, the heat warmeth the dew, bringing life, and I am she. When I opened my eyes my face was toward the setting of the sun, and a loud voice told me to go forth in the direction of my face and find my companions and there abide, and forthwith I have come." Then Klose-kur-beh with a loud voice of joy lifted his hands towards the noon-day sun, thanking the Great Spirit in fulfilling the promise. And immediately Klose-kur-beh walked to the brookside and there beheld a little animal swimming in the water. He called the little animal to him and the animal obeyed him, and

Klose-kur-beh slew the animal with sticks and brought it forth to his house of sticks and leaves and prepared the meat for a meal for himself and the woman, and a voice in the air came to their ears, saying: "It is not good to eat meat and blood together, therefore I will send fire unto you; take it and put it on the ground and put sticks on it so the sticks will burn, and put the meat on the fire so the blood will cook dry, and when it is cooked take and eat, this is good." After this saying, a cloud arose in the direction of the setting of the sun, which came fast with a loud noise, and with fire brightening the clouds. The clouds burst, and send forth a streak of fire, striking the top of the soft-wood tree that was standing by the brook-side, and the fire breaking the top of the tree, rolled around, following the grains of the tree, tearing the bark; and on the nakedness of the tree, a smoke arose, and there was a fire burning near the roots.

Klose-kur-beh immediately gathered all of the fire, put it on the ground with some sticks, which he made burn. He put the meat on the fire and cooked it. After it was cooled the two persons did eat, and Klose-kur-beh said it was good. On the morrow at the noon-day sun, a young man came unto Klose-kur-beh and No-ka-mi, and the young man's motions were very quick for he was yet young in age. Facing the cold land, he stood before them and said unto Klose-kur-beh: "I have come to abide with you and I have no other place to go, because I know no other persons but you. I have come to help you in all things. I am young in age, quick in my motion. I will be useful to you. I am small, but the body from whence I came is large, and there is no end to that body, therefore I will call you Nas-sar-sis,—my mother's brother." And Klose-kur-beh answered and said: "Natar-wun-sum,—my sister's son," and the young man said: "I owe my existence to the beautiful foam of the waters. The wind of the heavens blew, and moving the waters so that it rolled in great rolls so that the top broke, leaving the foam on top the water, and the noon-day sun shone on the foam and the heat of the sun warmeth the foam and the warmth bringeth life, and I am he. The wind of the heavens carried me to the land, and a loud voice told me to go forth in the direction of my face and find my companions and there abide. Knowing that when I opened my eyes my face was toward the cold land and I have come forth, I am your help. Klose-kur-beh lifted up his hands toward the noon-day sun, and giving thanks to the Great Spirit, immediately went to the brook-side, taking with him a fragment of the animal's meat and the threads of the bark of the soft wood tree which had been torn by the lightning, and tied the fragments on one end of the bark thread; he called loudly for the fishes to come, and three obeyed him,—one fish red, one white and one black—Klose-kur-beh casting the meat into the water, saying: "One of you, who is willing to become food for my children, bite the meat and I will draw you to the land, and you shall be food for my children." Immediately the red fish did bite the meat and Klose-kur-beh drew him unto the land, and Klose-kur-beh said: "The two fishes yet in the water are food for other men;" and

2

turning to the fishes, he commanded them to return to the deep water, and there stay until called forth by men, the color of their color, and the two fishes obeyed and returned to deep water. Without killing the fish with the sticks, No-ka-mi cooked it in the fire, and when it was cold the three did eat, and Klose-kur-beh called it good. When another morrow came, and when the sun was highest, another person came unto the three, whose motion was gentle, and brow fair. Who greeted all with down-cast eyes, saying "Ni-jun-duke"—My children, and Klose-kur-beh answered and said; "Nee-gar-oose"—Mother. The person was a young maiden. She opened her mouth, and with a soft voice said these words, "I have come to stay, and I have brought all the color of life on my brow; Love is mine, and I will give it unto you, and if you will love me, as I love you, and grant my wish, all the world will love me, even the beast will love me, and will steal my body because they love it. Strength is mine, and those who can reach me will get it. Peace is mine and I will bring content to the heart that seeks it; but woe unto the man, who does not heed its power, he is a brute. There will be many seventy times seven persons who shall share in it, therefore keep it pure. Because I have no other place to go, and I know no other but you. I have come; I am young in age and I am tender, yet my strength is great and I shall be felt all over the world, because I owe my existence to the beautiful plant of the earth, and as the evening and morning dew falleth on the leaf of the plant when the sun was highest and shining on it, the heat of the sun warmeth the dew, and the warmth brought life, and I am she. When I opened my eyes my face was toward the rising of the sun and a loud voice spoke unto me, saying, 'Go forth in the direction of thy face, and find thy companions.' Immediately I obeyed; because others are coming, we must prepare the way, so that all that come may abide with us." Immediately Klose-kur-beh lifteth up his hands toward the sun when it was highest and with a loud voice praised the Great Spirit for having fulfilled all the promises he had made unto him, and Klose-kur-beh bowed his head low giving four thanks to the Great Spirit, one toward the rising of the sun—one toward the setting of the sun—one toward the noon-day sun—one toward the cold land, and immediately went forth to the thick growth of bushes and from the branches of the bushes, picked Par-gun-sal,—nuts, and brought them forth to the young man and commanded him to break the nuts with Pen-nep-skole,—stones, so that the young maiden may eat. The young man obeyed, and the four persons did eat of the nuts; and before the sun's shadow was too far toward the rising of the sun, Klose-kur-beh bade the three to come forth and face the noon, and there join hands and give thanks to the Great Spirit, in the name of the substance that bore them; and the three obeyed, and the words of thanks repeated came from the mouth of Klose-kur-beh. Thus the first coming of the people to the Red-man's world began.

At this period Klose-kur-beh assigns the duties of each person, and the assignment was made according

to the coming of each. He says, "Because the substance that brought us to life is the substance of this
world, therefore we must always hold ourselves as a
part of the world, because we are substance of it. I
arose from the dust of the earth, I must see to it, so
that the earth may be clear of all obstacles, and the
land be our home, and a home for the people who will
come after us. We must not believe our thoughts if
they tell us we are to live always, because in one of
the seventy times seven nights the Great Spirit spake
unto me, saying, 'Man must not expect to live
always,' and on other nights the Great Spirit continued
upon the same subject, so all that was said to me, I am
able to say to you, and my words are many. While I
labor in purifying the land No-ka-mi will keep my
house and prepare the food for eating, and the young
man, because he is quick in motion, he shall go forth
and bring unto No-ka-mi all that he gets in hunting; he
shall bring it for food; he shall first kill the animal
with the bow made of hard wood; he shall bend the
wood, and the spring of the wood will have strength
so it will send forth the arrow and the bow shall have
power so that the arrow will have force to kill."

"The young maiden, because she is tender and with
fair brow;—she shall be the brightness of our house;
she shall welcome all that come to abide with us; and
because her strength is great, and must be felt all over
the land, she shall give it to those who come, because
none can abide without it. Strength is hers because
she is the seed of the world. Four kinds shall the
people see moving in this world; four seeds the Great

Spirit gave unto it. From one seed is man; from another seed are the beasts and animals; from another seed the fowl of the air, and from another the fishes of the water. Every seed shall bear after its kind. Because the Great Spirit made the man, in his own image, he will give unto him in due season the power over all others that come from the other seeds. But in the beginning, the Great Spirit gave greater strength to the beast than he did the man. This is done only to show that the world rests in His will, and the power of man and beast is subject to change; and the Great Spirit calls this wisdom, who said, 'If I give an endless power to one, he will claim it as his own and forget that it came from *Me*.' The Great Spirit said again, 'I will warn the one in power before I bring the change unto him. I have given the beast, the fowl, and the fish, greater strength than man. But a spirit from me has gone forth unto them, telling them, that I will give the greater power unto man, and in due season, each one shall, by the bidding of man lay down at his feet. Power is sweet and all shall struggle for it, and happy are they who find it. But a great sorrow and anger shall come unto those who lose it; therefore *beware*; and make it known among you that the beasts, fowl and fishes, are in great anger and seek your life. They are seeking an opportunity to show revenge by violence; therefore mingle not with them, but meet them only as enemies, until the change has been made."

After this the Great Spirit spoke again unto me, saying, "Great will be the period when the power

will change from beast to man ; but greater will it be,
when the power changes from *man* to *man*. Because
in changing the power from the beast to man I have
the man to do my work, but when the change is made
between man and man I shall have to do the work with
my own hands. There will be father, mother, sons
and daughters, yet all must be brothers and sisters ;
because all are from the dust, stone, water, and
the plants of the earth, and all live, are fed and
get strength from the same air brought by the wind
from heaven."

While yet the Great Spirit was speaking to me he
said this, "All living things shall know their kind,
and shall go in mates, and after that there will be in
the land great numbers ; yet each shall know his mate,
and because the man shall have power over all living
things it is good that he be mated. The man shall
be mate for the woman and the woman shall be mate
for the man, and on the morrow when the sun is highest, the man and the woman shall go forth to face the
sun, and the man shall give his right hand to the
woman, and the woman shall take his right hand with
her left hand and both shall bow towards the sun ;—
seven times shall they bow toward the sun on each
morrow ; and after that they shall be husband and
wife,—after the passing of seven suns they shall be
one flesh, and immediately shall the man walk seventy
times seven steps toward the noon, and there build a
house made of sticks and leaves ; the door shall be
toward the noon sun ; seven days shall he be building
the house ; and on the seventh day the woman shall go

forth among the soft wood trees and break the tender
boughs of the trees, and bring them to the house and
lay them on the ground for a bed for the husband and
the wife; the woman shall there abide with the man;
and on the morrow the man and the woman did go
forth to make the *bow*, and the man did make the
house, and the woman made the bed, and both lived
in the house.   After another seven days had passed,
Klose-kur-beh visited them and began to teach them
more.   He gave the man all the land south of the
house for his children, while Klose-kur-beh claimed all
the north land, because, he came from that way,—
he said to the man, "There will be no more come
to abide with me, and after I teach your children,
and   subdue the land, it will be good for me to
return to the north-land and there abide.   When I go
to the north-land No-ka-mi will go with me, no other
person shall go, and none shall know where I abide,
because when one goes too far towards my abiding
place he shall not live to get back; and as nature
feedeth ambition many will not be able to resist the
the temptation of gaining more of the world, but will
go forth toward me only to perish; yet others will not
take this warning but will follow those who have
perished, until the north-land shall no longer exist;
But before I go to the north-land the Great Spirit
charged me to teach you this—'When you are in
hunger, take your bow and go forth and kill such
animals as you need for food and bring them unto the
woman who shall prepare the meat for food, and you
shall prepare the skins to cover your bodies and bed.

I have many words to say, therefore I shall come
and teach you these same things on every seventh day,
and this day shall be one of the seventh. On the
other seventh days I shall repeat all my sayings so
you will be able to repeat them to your children and
your children to their children, until the things of the
world will get so sweet to the people they will forget
the words of the Great Spirit and shall begin to teach
their children only on things they see in the world.
When that day comes, I shall return from the north-
land to teach you more. Klose-kur-beh then said unto
the Woman, "You are to be the first mother of the
children that are to come, you shall bear unto your
husband seven sons and seven daughters and their children shall become seven tribes, and from these seven
tribes, many times seven tribes shall come until they
cover the land. After you shall have borne the seven
sons and seven daughters, a spirit will come to you, in
your sleep, and tell you what to do, so that you can
be with your children and their children while the earth
stands.

When first I met you all,—the first who came was
the *woman*, but with you, the first child you shall bear,
shall be born *man*, and the second shall be woman.
There shall be a man born, before every woman, and
the first born man, shall take unto himself a wife, who
shall be of the fourth born woman; the second shall
take the fifth; the third shall take the sixth; the
fourth shall take the seventh; the fifth shall take the
first; the sixth shall take the second, and the seventh
man shall take the third woman; it will not be good

for them, if they will not obey this order; because if
the first born man, take the first born woman for wife,
she will be too near kin unto him, and they shall be at
the head of a weak generation. So forget not my saying, because obedience is sweet and gives strength to
generations who practice it." Then Klose-kur-beh
said to the man, "Before I teach you many things, go
forth to the soft wood tree by the brook-side that has
been torn by the ball of fire; take up one fragment of
the wood that have been torn from the tree in your
right hand, and face the noon and dip the wood in the
water in remembrance of your origin, and bring the
wood to me. And because No-ka-mi owes her origin
to the stone, I have sent her after a fragment of the
stone, and because she is of the stone, knows the
nature of it, and will bring forth such is needed to do
our work." When the man had come with the wood,
No-ka-mi also came with the stone, and immediately
Klose-kur-beh began to break the stone with the fragment of the wood saying, "I shall make these things
out of stone, so that we, and the children to come after
us, shall have tools to use;" and Klose-kur-beh did
shave the stone into all kinds of tools for the people to
use. And said unto the man, "Take these implements of stone, and you shall share with me the
power given me by the Great Spirit. You shall be
able to cut the hard wood tree and make for yourselves
and those who come after you, bows to shoot with,
also vessels that will bear you upon the water.
Before I leave you to go to the north-land I shall
give you the same power I now have, so you also may

be able to shave the stone into tools as you have seen
me do this day. One particular duty above all I must
mention and you must obey; that is, you must teach
the people never to leave this land to seek other lands;
so when you make yourself a vessel let it be so made
that it will only be large enough to serve you on the
rivers and lakes, because when I first opened my eyes
I beheld large bodies of water all around the land
upon which we move and stand; and in the seventy
times seven nights the Great Spirit said unto me,
'There shall be other people live on the land as well as
your people.'"

And this I learned from the Great Spirit,—that he
made another man like me, but that he bade him go
toward the setting of the sun, and he shall some day
come to this land from the rising of the sun—There
must be still another man in some other part of the
world; because when I called forth the fishes as food
for man, three kinds obeyed—one red fish—one white
fish—one black fish. The white fish and the black fish
are yet in the deep water, waiting to be called forth by
men of their color. These men shall be one white and
one black. And further there shall be three seasons,
a season for each man. One shall be for the growing
of plants, and this growing season shall be pleasant to
mankind, because it will bring forth many beautiful
colors, pleasing to the eye. There shall be a season
when the plants shall be gathered as the people wants
them, and every plant shall show when it is ready to be
gathered, it will turn dark in color; after this
season has passed, the last season shall come,—a season

when everything must be prepared for its coming.   The
one who is not prepared for it shall suffer in many
ways; cold and hungry shall he be, because the season
that is to come shall destroy everything; therefore take
warning; when you see the plants taking in its beautiful
color, and the trees shake off their green leaves, then
the last season is at hand, then shall its breath be felt.
Even the rivers and the lakes shall close up its waters
to keep the fishes in the deep.   Then shall come the
last season in its white robe, which shall cover the
whole land and shall occupy it five moons.   All this
shall come once in every twelve moons.   The growing
season shall be the Red man's season.   The gathering
season shall be the Black man's season, and the cold
season shall be the White man's season.   The seasons
were divided by the Great Spirit, and because the Red
man obeyed the first teaching given unto him, he shall
enjoy a pleasant one.   And because the Black man did
not obey when told to look upon the earth when he
first opened his eyes, he shall always wait to follow
the bidding of his brother; and because the White man
wanted to stay on the land where he first opened his
eyes and wanted the Great Spirit to give him all he
beheld, the Great Spirit bade him go toward the setting
of the sun.   The Great Spirit saw that the man he had
made wanted the whole world, therefore he sent him to
chase the sun; when he comes to the great waters he
shall make large vessels, so he can chase the sun across
the great waters, because he wants all the world; he
shall slay his brother because he wants all things; he
shall know no one because he wants the power over all

the earth. The first born shall slay the next kindred to himself for the want of power and possession. Power and possession shall be so sweet to him, that it will turn his nature to disobedience; even the first woman shall disobey the Great Spirit, and bring death unto mankind,—who shall be sent forth to seek food· He will not heed the sayings and warnings of the Great Spirit but shall continue in the ways that he likes, until the Great Spirit shall be so provoked he will send a great rush of water, and all the bad shall be drowned,— but a few saved, who will continue to live good, and shall increase until they be like the sand of the earth; and shall be able to use all things for their convenience and comfort. Great men shall be put to rule, and the rulers shall be many; each ruler will want all the power over the others; this the Great Spirit will call bad, and the Great Spirit will come among them in the form of a man like unto themselves, and will stay among them, and teach them the way he wishes them to live. But their love of power will be so great they will slay the great spirit unto death. The Great Spirit will show them that man hath not the power to destroy him, and he shall arise before them, and shall go up beyond their reach. His teaching to them shall be hard to understand because they did not stop to listen to his words while he taught them. The Great Spirit who is so good, will show them that, revenge is not good, and he will let them occupy the land for the purpose of mending their ways. He will only say to them that He will never come to them again in peace and that they shall not come to Him until they come like the little babes.   A line shall be drawn between Himself and them—humiliation and obedience only will save them.   The sweetness of the earth and love of power will destroy them.   Before the day of destruction comes, this man shall have enjoyed all the power and possession he desires, and he shall have tasted the sweetness of the earth.   When he sleeps he shall sleep on a bed of flowers scented with roses, he need only reach forth his hand to grasp all things for his comfort ; he will draw things for his convenience from the water, from the air, and from deep down in the earth ; and the Great Spirit shall be looking on ; for this is the time that the man is about to forget the death of the Great Spirit—The man not having repented, is to dig a pit in the water, the air, and the earth, wherein he shall fall.   After he shall have dug these pits, then the Great Spirit shall show the man His power.   He shall shake the earth, because the substance of the water, air and earth have been drawn out, and used for comfort sake, and all these things have been left like the empty hornet's nest shall cave into these great pits, and the people shall fall into them, like the sand ; And the powerful man shall be no more—Then the Great Spirit shall call me forth, toward the noon sun, to teach you more.   The putting to death of the Great Spirit will come to pass, in a far off land.

CHAPTER II.

With the aid of May May, Klose-kur-beh destroyed the Serpent. — The Sea Voyage.

BECAUSE I make mention of the awful day coming you must not make yourself afraid, as the Great Spirit will not bring this upon you, or your children. It will always be plain to you that your brother and you are two; you are red, and he white. The Great Spirit has established His number with you both. His number with you is seven, while with your brother it shall be three, and because his numbers are few, he shall live fast, and pass away quickly; and because your numbers are many you shall live slow, and shall linger along while beyond your brother. All these bad things will come to pass across the big water, therefore I must warn you not to build large vessels that will bear you across, so that you will not have a hand in taking the life of the Great Spirit. When the Great Spirit sees that you obey this warning you will escape His wrath, and He will show you how much He loves you; He will cause your children to be born in the same form in which He made the first man. There will not be a child born deformed, neither will any be killed by lightning; they shall escape the floods and earthquakes, and when the beast bites you, you will not go crazy with him, though crazy he be; and when you

cut your hand or your foot, your jaws will not close up
like the beasts. These promises shall be with you as
long as you keep yourselves within the bounds of my
teaching. Knowing that many temptations will come
to you—you shall become weak in mind, and shall
want to believe some other teachings, it is well for me
to say to you, that the white man will feel it as a duty
to his children to seek new lands for them, and that he
will not rest until he finds the land the Great Spirit
gave unto you. He shall not pass away without first
having put his foot upon all the lands that have been
made; therefore look for him always.

The first sign of his coming shall appear to you in
the form of a swan towards the rising of the sun; this
shall be his bird and you shall know it, because it will
be white. If his coming proves an injury to your children, drive him away; and if the power given unto
you, bye and bye, is not strong enough send up a cry
to the north-land, and you shall get help; and when
the help comes he shall flee to his own land, and when
he has fled, all the fragments he has left behind him
you take and keep, and use it to protect your children,
because it shall be the first fragment of contention.

When he brings his women and children, he will
come to stay, and he shall want all the land, because
the land will be so sweet to him. The first that come
shall not want to allow his own kind to share with
him; they shall slay one another for the possession
of it. Take no hand in their fights, because the Great
Spirit did not make the land for brothers to fight for;
He made it for love's sake.

Woe unto you when the temptation overpowers you and you take hand in his fights, because he shall have the way that he can put you in front of him, and you shall receive all the blows and be slain for his gain; and the two brothers shall make peace between themselves over your body that has been slain for the land because you have forgotten my teaching.   I must say to you, watch him closely, because the repentance he is to undergo is great, and he will ask you to help him repent, and he will say to you that the "Great Spirit died for him," he will show you the things that caused the death of the Great Spirit and he will teach you to bow down* to these things; and bow you may; but never forget that the Great Spirit is in the air, in the sun, moon, and in all things which your eyes can see.—Here the teaching of Klose-kur-beh ended.

I shall now enter into the details of his works. First he made the woman to select a hard wood tree for him to cut, and he went forth, and began to cut the tree into pieces with the stone implement he had made; he cut this only to show the man how the tools must be used, and then he gave the implement to the man and bade him to go forth, and make for himself things he needed; in making the necessaries of life, he told him to take the skin off the white wood tree, and make for himself a vessel that will bear him upon the water.   And said unto the man I shall now clean the earth of all obstacles, and shall also continue to make for you and your children, all the tools of stone until such time a power be given you, to make them yourselves. Now when you make the bow to shoot with make an arrow also, and make it so that the end next toward the animal be pointed; you shall burn the end so it shall be hard, and when you send it forth it will penetrate into the body and the animal shall fall dead so that you can prepare it for food. Fish you can not shoot with a bow and arrow; therefore you must kill a bird, and take from the bird's breast next to the neck, a small bone you shall find which is bent, and having two prongs,—rub one prong upon a stone so it will wear to a sharp point; and you shall strip the bark of a small bush of the Wik-a-bee kind, and work it into fine strings, and twist the strings so it will make a long line, and the line you shall fasten unto the blunt end of the bone, and you shall cut a small pole of the hard wood tree, and fasten the other end of the line on to the small end of the pole, and you shall put fragments of meat on the sharp point of the bone, and go and cast the meat into the water, and the fish shall bite the meat and shall pull the meat, line and pole, then draw him unto the land. And when the time comes that you need a vessel to bear you upon the water, you shall first cut from the soft wood tree, strips of it so small you can easily bend, and the strips shall be in length according to the vessel wanted; both ends shall come to a point, so it will cut the water when you make it go. The vessel must be propelled by the power of your arms and hands with a paddle made from the hard wood tree.

Some thin strips of the soft wood you shall shave out for lining; there shall be two linings, one length-

3

wise, and one cross-wise; after these are ready you shall level and smooth the ground, and lay the bark of the white wood tree on the ground, and cut the bark on each side, so you can shape it to a point on each end, and lay the top frame on the bark and then turn up the side flaps of the bark closely to the frame, and you shall sew the side flaps together with strips of the roots of the soft wood tree, and you shall make holes through the bark, with the tail of the shell fish So-ba-qui-dole-beh, "horse shoe," that you find on the sea shore; after sewing up the seams you shall raise the frame to the top of the bark and sew the bark on to the frame; it will then be ready to receive the two linings; and the seams you shall close up with the sap of the pitch wood tree called Puk-go, "pitch," so that the water will not enter into the vessel; after this is done your vessel will be ready to bear you upon the water.

Klose-kur-beh said, now that you have all your "Ar-wa-kur-gan," (tools) to make "Ar-quee-dun," (canoe) "Tur-by," (bow) "Par-queh," (arrow.) You can make all these things when you want them, and when the time comes, and before your sons shall take unto themselves wives, each man shall go forth into the forest, with the bow and arrow and eat what he takes in hunting, and shall cover his body with the skins. Seventy times seven moons shall he be absent from your people; he shall then return and take unto himself a wife. In seven days when the sun is highest I will come again to repeat to you these same things. Seventy times seven, shall I come, but before I leave you this day, I will say, "The first born you shall call "Na-mun," (son) and the second shall be called "Na Doose" (daughter.)

Here Klose-kur-beh left the husband and wife to themselves, only returning every seventh day to teach them until the allotted time had been fulfilled; after which the man and wife went their way, as well as Klose-kur-beh and No-ka-mi, so nothing remarkable can be said of the man, during a long period. There is much to be said of the woman; the details of which will be given later.

First we will examine the works of Klose-kur-beh, because it is clear that his mission was to clean the whole earth. He now goes to work to subdue the animals and beasts, so that man will not have much trouble in conquering them afterwards. In those days as has been said before, the beast sought after man's life, not only devouring him when they met, but also roving through the forest seeking after him. The man and woman were in constant fear lest they be devoured. Klose-kur-beh, who saw the condition of things, went forth to meet all the ferocious roving beasts; he called each one to him and these that obeyed, he asked if they were willing to become small; and all that came with willingness he transformed into small animals and covered them with fine fur. Those that hesitated and lingered behind, he changed smaller and with coarse hair. One animal when asked if he was willing to be changed answered "No," and immediately made a leap upon the branches of the tree, and looked down upon Klose-kur-beh from the high

branches and said, "When man leaps from branch
to branch as I, then shall I submit to his bidding."
Then Klose-kur-beh said, "Because from the branches
of the tree you choose to bark at man—be it so—but
as you are to leap from branch to branch your great
weight will break the branches down therefore, you
need to become small so you can travel on the branches
of the trees," and immediately the animal became
small and Klose-kur-beh called him "Miqu-go-a"
(squirrel.)   When Klose-kur-beh looked around he saw
a very large animal, much larger than those near him,
and the form of his body was not like the others—his
back was the shape of the half moon with a very small
head for the body, with large but thin ears hanging
down each side of his head; eyes and mouth small and
the upper lip so long he could reach out with it seven
paces and up among the branches of the trees; and
there were two long horns on each side of his long lip.
When Klose-kur-beh called him he would not answer,
but would swing his long lip to the right, then left, up,
then down, with great force, shaking his head each
time.   Seven times Klose-kur-beh called him forth—
seven times did the animal show violence, and after
seven times repeating this manner of disobedience, said
to Klose-kur-beh, "No, I will not go forth to man and
humble myself to obey his bidding; I will never obey
the bidding of my enemy as long as he can not show
the power and strength that I can.   Even the trees
bend when I touch them; I can break the branches with
my long lip and tear up the earth when I choose; and
when I meet your children, they can only save them-

selves by running out of my way; and woe unto them
that I can reach with my lip, I will dash them against
my teeth so that my teeth will go through them.
Seven of your children can I hang on my two teeth
and go my way to meet more. Their weapons I do
not fear, because my skin is so thick and hard even
the hair will not grow out of it; and my flesh so deep
that covers my life, there can nothing reach that life
which can be brought against it by your children;
therefore I will repeat and say no. Enemies we entered
the land and enemies let us live in it; man, go your
way, and I will go my way." At this saying Klose-
kur-beh paused with sorrow; immediately a spirit
of thought came unto him, and he said to the animal—
"Because your body is great you will not come to the
bidding ¯of man—your pride lay in the thickness of
your skin and the great depth of your flesh.   This
is vanity, "pride will stand only for a moment," and
woe unto you "Par-sar-do-kep-piart."—mammoth, for
in a little while, your pride will fall with your body.
This will show my children that there is a power
somewhere which is far greater than your power that
can protect them from any violence you can press
against them.   There will be no need of teaching a
lesson to those that will come after you, because there
will be none, because when the power does its work,
it will be final, none of your kind will escape, but
will all perish alike.   My children shall stand around
and gaze upon your bones; and the bones will last
as long as the world stands, but your skin and flesh
that gives you so much pride will never be seen

by any of my children," and immediately a dark
cloud arose from the setting of the sun approaching
very low toward where Klose-kur-beh and the animal
was standing, and a loud voice came unto Klose-kur-
beh, saying, "Depart from the spot immediately,—
you and the animals that obey you, because the
howling of the brute will be great; but greater will
be the roaring of the heavens, to drown his howls;"
and Klose-kur-beh obeyed the warning and departed
with all the animals that obeyed him, and immediately
the clouds began to roar very loud all over the heavens
and the lightning shooting in every direction, and the
howling of the animal was heard no more. When
the clouds passed away there was a great calm; and
when the night came, the heavens at the north land
began to turn into a beautiful white, and the white
began to dance among the stars of the heaven, dancing
toward the noon, until the white covered all the
heavens, and Klose-kur-beh called it, "Nee-bur-
bann;—night dawn," or the northern lights.

After this great event Klose-kur-beh rested seven
moons; and after resting seven moons he went
forth to clear the water, and to clear the rivers
and lakes of its obstruction. To do this it was necessary that he should make for himself a canoe of bark,
and to make it in the same manner that he taught the
man. After he had made the canoe, and put it in the
water he went forth upon the water to find obstructions.
He found branches and roots of trees in all the rivers
and lakes so that the canoe could not pass, because
every branch that had fallen into the water, had more

life than the ones on the land, the water gave to it more life than the land did; when he began to tear up the branches, the parts that lay next to the bottom had sprouted and rooted fast on to the bottom; but with the aid of the spiritual Power, he was able to dislodge every branch. Not only the branches that lay at the bottom of the rivers sprouted, but the virtue of the water gave great growth to them so that they reached from one shore to the other shore of the rivers; likewise he found things the same upon all the lakes. Although having such spiritual power, that had he wished, he could with one stroke of his hand remove all obstructions; but no,—such was not his object; he wanted to show the man that he must not always wait for spiritual help, but do the things with his own labor, only appealing to spiritual power when necessity required it. Therefore when the allotted seventy times seven moons had ended, his work was not finished, and he marvelled with a great sorrow at the slowness of his work. Immediately there came a voice from the heavens saying, "Marvel not man, at the slowness of your work, because you must know, that the work of man under the water must not be the same as on the land; man must not be hasty when he works under the water, because if he be hasty he will only bring death unto himself. Therefore do your work slowly so that when your work is done it will last forever. Therefore you are allowed seven times the allotted time of seventy times seven to do your work, so marvel not, but go on with good cheer because this work must be done now, and after it is finished nature will not obstruct the waters, and no more such work be wanted done. Hereafter when man works under the water it will be only to find the things he had dropped there," and Klose-kur-beh obeyed the voice from Heaven, and went on cheerfully with his work. How long a time it took him to finish the work he seemed to have kept that to himself.

All these things Klose-kur-beh did without having a war with anything until his labors were completed. But upon returning to his people from his work by way of the sea he found the waters very dark in color and the stench of it was great, because there had been a great calm over all the sea, following the destruction of the "Par-sar-do-kep-piart,"—Mammoth, and the danc- ing of the "Nee-bur-bann,"—Northern lights, conse- quently the waters became stagnant and foul. And as he moved along he saw a serpent at a long distance, as it lay on the surface of the dark water. Upon nearing the monster, it raised its head and began to run out its firelike tongue rapidly at him; by this action he was well aware that this was another deadly enemy; so he steered his canoe directly for the monster and the serpent reared up in a fearful manner and seemed ready to crush the canoe and the man, but at that moment "May-May,"—"Red headed wood pecker" flew between the man and the serpent and danced in the air for awhile, seemed undecided which way to fly until it saw the serpent make for the man, then the bird flew toward the man and lit upon the bow end of the canoe and said to him, "Be quick and take your bow and shoot the arrow at the smallest part of the reptile's body," and Klose-kur-beh obeyed the bird and shot the arrow but it only rebounded without doing the intended execution, and the bird flew, picked up and brought back the arrow, saying, "Aim nearer the tail," the arrow went again only to rebound as before. Six times this was repeated and six times met with the same results, but on the seventh, the bird flew in advance of the arrow and with its beak pointed to Klose-hur-beh where to aim, Klose-kur-beh obeyed and sent the arrow swiftly to the spot very near the end of the tail; this broke the serpent's back bone, which caused him to recoil in death.

In the excitement caused by this determined effort on the part of both man and serpent while struggling for an ascendency over each other, Klose-kur-beh did not notice what was following the conquest just gained, until "May-May,"—wood-pecker, called his attention to it, and upon looking around he beheld that the whole sea was in blood, and the body of the serpent just slain laying on the surface, its head toward the land, and many times seventy smaller reptiles coming out of its mouth, all heading for the land; May-May said, "Let them go in peace, they can never grow large enough to do you harm as long as they stay on the land," and Klose-kur-beh did let them go in peace as May-May commanded, and after these sayings May-may wanted Klose-kur-beh to put a mark upon him for his services in helping the man complete his work of subduing the earth. In obedience to May-May's wishes, Klose-kur-beh turned his canoe which was then heading for the north land, and made the bow point toward the noon, looked up, and with his right hand dipped the head of the arrow into the sea of blood and put the blood on May-May's head as a mark of true friendship. When this was done, the whole sea became clear and pure, and May-May said, "Because the serpent has chosen the sea as the battle ground to fight the man, and as its blood been spilt in the sea, let the water be bitter to taste so that no man or beast shall want to drink it,"—and it was so. After this May-May, the bird, said to Klose-kur-beh, "In friendship we came unto the world, and in friendship let us live in it. Because you did not call me nor any of my kind when you were changing all the animals and beasts—making them smaller, I have been watching the movements of your enemies, and I have seen that the serpent was very mad when the power of the Great Spirit destroyed the existence of "Par-sar-do-kep-piart" and his wrath has been so great that he came here where he thought no power could reach him because when the rush of clouds and wind comes he can sink himself to the bottom out of harm's way, and here he has been waiting many times seven moons for your coming, and has held this calm over the sea which followed the destruction of Par-sar-do-kep-piart and the dancing of the heavens, so that the sea water became stagnant; but now the monster is gone and his dead body you will see no more. And because the way of the whole land and sea is clear I must depart from you for awhile ; you go your way and after which let your kind put on his head and body the covering of me and my kind ; it will make him proud because it showeth the greatness of our friendship. There will be no more trouble between man and beast ; your work is now complete, you can go your way to your children who need your teaching," and May-May immediately flew away towards the setting of the sun.

When Klose-kur-beh turned the bow of his canoe toward the north land he beheld not the body of the serpent on the surface of the water, but instead there was a beautiful ripple all over the sea caused by the gentle breeze from the direction of the setting sun, to where May-May had flown. It was here, when Klose-kur-beh for the first time felt tired; May-May going away made him feel lonely and he wanted to see his own people. When night came this same lonely feeling was still upon him, he prepared a place for a night's rest. After the darkness had come and before laying down to sleep, to cheer himself, Klose-kur-beh did sing. When this was done, the seven trees that stood nearest bent their tops down and listened to the singing of Klose-kur-beh, and when the singing was over, the largest of the seven straightened its body up and said, "How grateful the heart of man ought to be when he can bring cheer to himself by singing when lonely. When my kind and I sing, we sing in distress; when the fury of the winds shake our limbs we sing in wailing,—our roots are many and strong and cannot move to avoid the fury of the heavens. We stand and wait for whatever befall us. Because you can move at your pleasure do not linger here, but on the morrow when the sun rises take your canoe, and with your companion go forth toward the sun, heed not the moving of the sun during the day, but keep that same course that you take from here and keep it seven days and seven nights, and on the seventh, when the sun is highest, you will come to a swift water which will turn

your canoe toward the noon, and the swift water will
bear you, your canoe and companion very fast in
the direction you ought to go. Seven moons you will
be borne that way, and after the seven moons have
passed take your paddle and turn the bow of your
canoe toward the setting sun and in seven days from
that time you will find land and trees. When you find
land it will be like this land and the trees the same as
we. Your work will then be complete because you
shall then have found that there is a spirit in all things,
and where there is a spirit there is knowledge, and
where there is knowledge there is power, and as there
is knowledge in us, we, the seven trees, will show you
the power that is in us and will smooth the way for
you the whole time of your journey. When you reach
the swift water call it "Etto-chi-psi-tuk,—Gulf Stream."
But you must not claim it for your convenience alone,
because this swift water was made for the convenience
of three men,—one red, one white and one black man.
The course of the current will change four times ; when
the time comes that either of these three men wish to
use it will change its course to suit his convenience,
—a course for the red man, a course for the white man
and one for the black man. After each has had a share
it will return then to the same course as you will find
it seven days hence. On the morrow when you depart
from here, take nothing for food because it will be
brought and laid before you each day by your faithful
friends. When you depart on the morrow put a mark
on me so that you may know me when you return,
because from here you must return to your people.
When you reach the end of your great journey on the

swift water and have found land and trees, turn to the
north land which will bring you back to here, and from
here you will know which way to find your people."
After this saying, the other six trees bent back straight
and all was silent and Klose-kur-beh went to sleep.
When the morrow came and when the first dawn broke
forth to tell that the sun was coming, a loud barking
of an animal was heard coming from the direction of
the setting sun. Klose-kur-beh answered it seven
times, when the animal came shaking its tail, and with
ears dropped down on the side of his head, and having
in his mouth large fragments of meat which he laid at
the feet of the man, and said, "I have come to stay
with you, I shall stay where and when you stay,
and I shall go when and where you go, When all the
animals got together after all the fear had passed at the
destruction of "Par-sar-do-kep-pi-art," we all lay down
to talk about your good heart in saving us from such awful
destruction, and I was sent to be your companion.
Knowing that after all trouble will have passed away,
man's feeling shall then come to him ; there shall be a
time for him to weep, and a time for him to laugh, a
time to be happy and a time to be lonely, but in time
of loneliness you will have a great comfort in me, because when you are in hunger I will find game for you
to kill that you may be filled. I have brought this as
the food for myself because before I started we all of us
heard the trees talk with you. I know where you and
I are going this day, although the food I have brought
is only enough for a little while, yet it will last during
our goings, though long it be. And as there is a spirit
in all things, the united spirit of myself and those that

have sent me will have power in this matter. I fear
not hunger." And when Klose-kur-beh heard this his
loneliness left him and he said to the animal, "welcome
Arl-moose,"—dog, Then the man got the canoe ready
to start, and while waiting for the sun to rise he put a
mark upon the tree, chipping off the bark on the side
toward the rising sun, while the Arl-moose divided the
fragments of meat of the "Ta-mar-queh—beaver," took
the liver and buried it deep in the ground in front of the
spot on the tree, saying, "The nature of me and my
kind will help us much in finding this spot." Then the
dog took the other meat and the tail of the beaver and
carried it forth to the canoe and laid it therein and
carefully covered it with the "Kus-kul-siarl,—sea-
weed."

When the sun arose they started on their journey in
that direction and kept that course paying no attention
to the moving of the sun, and when the sun was
highest May-May came to them with a load of food and
water for the man which he laid before him, saying,
"Eat and drink and be filled," and after May-May had
departed on his journey back, Klose-kur-beh took up
the food and called it "Pun-Nuk,—Ground Nuts" and
did eat of it, and drank the water that was in the
vessel which he called "Weeh-po-lark-sun-suk,—Pitcher
plant," and Klose-kur-beh called it good. On the
morrow at the same time there came two May-May's
who brought food and water for the man, and when
the third day came three May-May's came, and brought
the same kind of food, and on the fourth day, four
May-May's came with the same, but this time two
"Weeh-po-lark-sun-suk" were brought. On the fifth

day, five May-May's came, and on the sixth, six May-May's came, and on the seventh, seven came which passed the canoe and made a circle, so that their coming to the canoe was from the direction of the rising sun, and the head one of the flock said to the man, "This day we came to you from another direction because it is not good for you to eat one kind of food always. There is much in the earth which is good for man to eat, therefore on the morrow there will be a change made. This day your course will be changed toward your right hand and your journey will be toward the noon, and in that direction you will go to the end of time which the trees have commanded you." After this saying the May-Mays' departed, leaving the man to eat his meal. Klose-kur-beh saw that each time he eat his meal the dog also ate his, but would only eat about half of the beaver's tail and laid away the other part for the next meal, and would cover it up carefully each time with the sea weed, and Klose-kur-beh noticed that each time when the dog uncovered his food it was whole, the same as it was before he began to eat of it. And while they were eating, the canoe reached the swift water which immediately turned it toward the noon and bore it very fast in that direction, and when the morrow came, when the sun was highest, the seven May-Mays came again bringing to the man a different kind of food which they laid before him, and immediately flew away. Klose-kur-beh saw it was a different kind of food which was taken from under the ground, and he called it "See-pun,—roots of the red lily," which afterwards became a great dish among the children of the red man. In

drifting along in this swift water he saw seven kinds of
fish and water animals. The first one seen he called "Ar-
kiqu,"—Seal, the next was the "Poo-da-peh,"—Whale;
then came the "Sur-bid-yar-maqu,"—Grampus, "See-
gar-lur-dee,"—Shark, came next, "Choos-ka-ba-so,—"
Porpoise, was also seen, "Noo-kar-mavu,"—Codfish,
came next, then came the seventh which he called
"Mur-mur-lar-maqu,"—Mackerel. No more fish were
noticed and no more named, and on each day his food
was brought to him. On every seventh day a change
of food was brought, there being only three vegetable
kind, the rest was in berries and fruit. In the first
part of his southern trip berries were brought, and toward the end of it, fruit and plums, and at the very
last was the vegetable again, with which he was kept
until the end of his voyage. The berries were
"M'skik-wee-min-sark,"—Strawberries, then the "Sar-
tarl,"—Blueberries, also the "Ka-pus-kee-mi-nuk,"—
Raspberries, and "Ars-paqu-sall," — Huckleberries,
"Arspump-squa-mi-nal,"—Gooseberries, and the "Chi-
loom-nal,"—Grapes, were brought, also the "Ar-do-ho-
do-arl"—Bananas. The May-Mays also brought "War-
sar-wa-si-sall,"—Oranges, and at last the "Arp-cha-da-
sarl,"—Potatoes, and he said, "As this kind of food will
be the most common, yet the principal food for man, we
will bring no other kind as you are soon to reach the
land, after which you can gather your own food.
When the allotted time for sailing had passed, when
the sun was highest, the May-Mays came with the same
kind of food, and after laying the same before the man
he said, "We will now all of us take leave and bid
adieu to the swift water, and when we are up high and

have taken our course, you and your companion turn
the bow of your canoe toward the right hand and follow
us, keep that same course until you reach the land.   As
we leave the swift water, we must first show our
reverence to the trees for their goodness in keeping
the waters quiet during your long voyage."

Immediately all the May-Mays arose, first going toward the north land, then turning toward the right,
toward the rising sun, then to the noon, and again
turning to the right, heading to the direction of the
setting sun, and one bird sang out, "Pess-aqu,—one,"
which caused all the birds to turn again to the right
and fly in the same circle as before.   Again the leader
counted, saying "Niss,—two," which caused them to
take another turn, and another circle was made, each
time going higher, and when the counting place was
reached "Narss—three" was counted and another circle
was made, and "Eaoo,—four," was counted and every
time a circle was made a count was taken of it, "Nun,
—five," Na-qua-ters,—six," "Tur-par-wurs,—seven,"
and on the seventh circle the birds were quite high in
the air, and continued on their way to the setting sun.

Klose-kur-beh turned his canoe to the right and followed the May-Mays which soon flew out of his sight.
For seven days he kept that course—each noon his food
and water was brought to him.   On the seventh day
when the sun was rising, only one May-May came who
after laying the food before the man said, "This day I
have done all my work for your sake and when night
comes, you will rest your body on the land among the
trees, and because the trees have commanded you to go
forth and find; the living water which the Great

3

Spirit has made for man's convenience, so when the
night comes when you take your rest, before going
to sleep, pour all the water that is still remaining
in the "Weeh-po-lark-sun-suk," around the roots of
the largest tree seven times ; and all the trees will
rejoice because this will be your thanksgiving and
you will have given all that you have, and each morning when you have risen, go on your way toward the
north-land and find your people ; I will come no more ;
and he flew away leaving the man and dog to finish
the voyage.   Klose-kur-beh watched the bird, who
flew away very low and he could see fishes jump up
out of the water as the bird was flying past, but May-
May flew so fast no fish could catch him ; and while yet
he was watching the bird and as the May-May flew out
out of his sight he saw beyond, the dark specks of the
land ; and when night came he was on it, and immediately prepared a place to rest for the night, and before
going to sleep did pour all the water he had around
the roots of the largest tree as May-May had commanded.

When morning came the dog got up and shook himself and said "I have eaten the last of my food, I took
it while you were in your sleep, and this day my work
for your sake begins ; whatever you want I shall find,
but you must prepare it to your own liking—Give me
not of it, but give me the crumbs, that is my portion."
Straightway the dog went until he came near to the
edge of the water and there put his head down and
began to dig the wet earth with his two paws, and
soon brought out of it a shell fish and brought it to
the man and laid it at his feet saying, "Take and eat,

and be filled," and Klose-kur-beh did break the shell
and did eat the "Aiss"—Clam.   After this was done
the two started on their journey toward the north-land,
keeping their course very near the land along the
coast.

CHAPTER III.

Klose-kur-beh's hunting.—The first mother changed into corn and tobacco.

NOTHING can be said of events during this long
northern journey, nor the exact time it took to accomplish it, only that when Klose-kur-beh reached his
people he told them it took many seven times seven
moons journey from the time he turned to north land
to find them.   So by his statement that the swift water
must have carried him very fast southward.   He also
mentioned having found the different kinds of food the
same as the May-May brought to him while on his journey southward, and how he gathered and lived on the
same after turning northward.   One incident which was
brought about by his companion, the dog, he spoke of
with much emphasis, and described it minutely, and
designated the place, and told the people he had
put a mark on the spot which would stand as long as
his people existed.   The following was his story, "One
day when we, (meaning himself and the dog,) had arrived at a place of a high mountain whose slopes run
down to the waters' edge, the dog, who was asleep in
the canoe, while I was paddling, got up, began to

breathe hard, putting his nose up in the air as if to catch
the freshness of it, and when he finally turned his head
toward the high mountain, in which position he held
himself for a long while, turned to me and said, 'Master,
here in this part of the north land man must needs have
some meat to eat because such he will find from here
north,—berries and fruit are good in their season and
places, but the time is coming when these will *lose*
their season; therefore when night comes, get your
bow and arrow ready for using, because at the breaking
of day to-morrow I will go up on the high mountain
we have just passed :—there is now feeding on the
bark of the mountain trees, moose, whose meat is good
for you and your kind and me and my kind, the virtue
of which gives strength to the body and makes the
heart glad to those who are fortunate enough to get it,
which will always be valued highly by your people
because it can be saved to keep many days, yea,
many moons.   On the morrow, before the sun is
highest I will drive one to you and when I do this,
shoot and kill.   After you have killed the animal you
shall immediately open his body : the belly you shall
open with your stone knife and the intestines you shall
give me, not from your hand to my mouth, but throw
it in front of me, because this is my portion and that
will be the way you will give it me.   If my saying is
not obeyed I will lose all the nature of my kind.   If I
get fat on the best part of the animal in common with
you, then the power of smelling the sweet meat of the
animal will be taken away from me, so beware and
give me what belongs to me.'"   When night came the

two companions rested, and when the next dawn came
the man awoke from his sleep and upon looking around
for his companion found him not, he beheld that the
dog's bed was vacant; immediately he got ready his
stone knife, bow and arrow, and in a little while he
heard the barking of his dog on the mountain. The
sound of the barking indicated that the dog was going
toward the water, and in another moment he saw the
animal swiftly running among the trees and bushes and
then came out of them and straightway he made for
the water, and into it he went. When he reached it
he began to swim across the water toward the other
land, and the dog also came out, but instead of going
into the water, ran on the shore, passed the animal
and kept on his way until he reached a point nearest
the other land, when he also went in, and swam so
fast that he reached it before the animal did; the dog
ran along the shore in front of the animal and would
not let him land, and when the man saw this he took.
his canoe and other things, went forth to get near the
animal so to kill it, and when he had come in front of
it, the animal saw that the man and the dog had reached
the shore before him, turned to go to the other land;
when the man saw what the animal was doing, he
followed it and just before reaching the other land came
upon it and with bow and arrow did slay the animal
and brought the body out of the water on to the land.

Upon looking around he beheld his dog afar off sitting on a point of land waiting for his portion. So in
a moment more he did cut the belly of the animal open
with a sharp stone knife and took out the contents and

did throw the intestines to his dog who was sitting
afar off—and said when he was doing this—"Let this
day put a mark on the place of my doings."—After
saying this he went to work to cut the animal and took
such parts as he needed for food. He did take the
fore part and left the other part for a mark, so that his
people might know where he made his first hunt for
the large animal. Upon doing this he took out the
"Oos-squon,"—Liver, and laid it beside the animal's
body, and then called the other part "Oo-kar-chi,"—
Hind part, after which he said, "These things needs
be here to mark my works and it shall be so, and the
mark shall stand as long as my people exist; and
immediately that part of the animal became stone, and
the intestines also left a mark across the water from
one shore to the other which was a long way. Some
parts of the intestines which he threw at his dog,
dropped down very near the spot where the body of
the animal lay and the other part reached near where
the dog was sitting so that the whole part did not
break or disconnect but strung along the whole distance which can' now be seen, resembling the intestines
of an animal, with its white fat and blood on the ledges
near the moose body, coming out at where the dog is.—
All along the whole distance this mark can now be
seen; according to the modern measurments and reckoning a distance of seven miles; these intestines lay
along the bottom of the sea which can be seen, wherever
the water is shallow enough so the bottom can be seen;
they lay on the ledges and on the large and small rocks
the whole way. When Klose-kur-beh had put the fore

part of the moose in his canoe and upon looking up to
see the dog he saw there were three—seeing this he
departed immediately toward them, but upon nearing
the spot discovered that the other two were stone
resembling in form, two dogs. When his mistake
became known to him he marvelled much and said,
"This is very strange. But man must take warning
that in all his works, his plans must needs, at times
be changed. I have made my plan to have my dog turn
into stone and leave it here to mark the place with the
other marks. But for this sudden change in my vision—
taking two stones for two dogs—making three dogs in
number when really there was but one, causes me to move
with more caution. Therefore I must change my plan so
that instead of letting my dog turn into stone to mark
this place, I shall let the two stones stand for a mark
and they shall stand during the pleasure of the people
whose number has been established to three. So he
called his dog into the canoe and resumed his journey.
When the hour came to prepare for a meal he turned
his canoe up into a small river, but finding rapids so
great he concluded not to ascend further than to the
foot of the rapids with the canoe, and wishing to mark
the spot where he first cooked his meal after killing
large game on his returning journey, took out some
meat and carried it to the head of the falls. Not having a kettle to cook his meat and as he wished to cook
the meat in water that flowed into the place where the
game was killed, he selected a place near the head of
the falls and dug out a place in the solid rock with his
hands—a hollow place—so it held water—he then

made a vessel out of birch bark with which he carried
water from the river to fill the stone kettle. While he
was absent getting the water the dog also began to dig
another hole in the ledge with its paws.; seeing on his
return what the dog had done, caused him to enquire
of the dog why he was digging the hole? The dog
replied that it was not good for man and dog to eat out
of the same dish. At this Klose-kur-beh said "There
will be no need for man and dog to eat out of the same
dish because you have already established a form in
which you shall receive the meat from the hand of man.
In the beginning of our journey north you declared to
me that when meal time came you would ask for the
fragments of the meal be cast before you. Let
this be the rule just as you have requested." At
this the dog stopped digging and laid down waiting for
the fragment from the man's meal. After getting all
things ready for cooking and having placed the water
and meat in the same kettle, Klose-kur-beh took two
fragments of dead and dry wood and facing the sun
rubbed the two sticks together until a blaze came, from
which he made a large fire and heated stones and put them
into the kettle; and the water did boil so that he was
able to cook his dinner. After eating the meal the
man and the dog returned to the canoe and resumed
their journey, leaving the two stone kettles in the
ledge as a mark where the first meal was cooked after
killing the first large game.

Nothing more can be said until the place from which
the two started was reached, the morning they took
their southern trip. Upot reaching the place Klose-

kur-beh was almost at a loss to find the exact spot, but the dog went directly to the spot and dug up the fragments of meat that he had buried there the morning they started, and the dog did eat the meat. This ended the sea journey.

When night came the man and the dog slept on the same ground where the man slept previous to the sea voyage ; and early on the morrow, after carefully laying away the canoe started on the overland journey to the man's people ; the dog leading the way. It took them only seven times seven suns to reach the people, and when it was known that Klose-kur-beh had returned, there was great rejoicing, and as the news spread many came from afar to greet him. He found that during his absence the people had multiplied very much. But he had no difficulty in finding No-ka-mi in the extreme northern part of the land inhabited by the people.

And here Klose-kur-beh began to make the stone implements for his people, because there had been a division ; the people had divided themselves into clans.

As soon as the news of the return of Klose-kur-beh reached the ears of the first mother of the people, she became very much agitated and her action gave much alarm ; nothing seemed to give her relief, and she showed a discontented mind day after day. She was yet fair, and it seemed that in all those years which were many, since she became the mother of the first child, her age had not changed ; she looked much younger than many of her off-springs, and the husband retained his age equally as well. Both being yet young, the love that existed between them was great ;

so when the man saw his wife in such a discontented
state it grieved him much. He used every means to
find out what brought such a discontent to his wife,
but all his efforts failed. He loved his wife so much
he thought it was out of place to ask her any questions
so concluded to wait for further developments. But
his waiting was all in vain; instead of the contentment
he had hoped for, the discontentment was on the increase and had got to such a stage that the wife absented
herself from his presence as the sun neared the noon
line each day, and remained away until the shadows
would be far toward the rising sun. Finally it had
such an effect upon his mind that he lost all control over
his patience, which soon reduced his manhood to such
an extent that the sense of honor left him, and he
determined to watch his wife. By careful watching
for a long time he discovered the direction she took in
going and would return the same way. He resolved
to make further discoveries, so one day just before
the time came for her return, he went and hid himself
near a river at a point where he could scan its banks
for a long distance. His patient waiting was rewarded
at last by seeing her coming to the opposite bank,
cheerfully singing as she entered to ford the river.
While her feet were in the water she seemed to be in a
very happy mood, there was brightness in her coun-
tenance, and he beheld something trailing behind her
right foot which appeared like a long green blade.
Upon reaching the shore she stooped down and with
her right hand picked off the trail, cast it into the
water and the thing floated away. As soon as she had

cast the blade from her, the same down cast look spread over her fair brow and with that look she went her way towards home. Soon after the woman had gone, the man came out from his hiding place and immediately began to search for the trail that had been cast into the water which he readily found lodged among the rocks below. Upon examining the thing it proved to be a long green blade of some strange plant, the like of which he had never seen before. While thus holding the blade in his hands a sense of honor returned to him and immediately he put the blade into the water and only gazed upon it while it floated away. Honor and patience having returned unto him he was ready to undergo any and every thing if only he could get the woman to tell him what would bring happiness to her. He resolved to gain her confidence by love, although this had failed in times past, but he made up his mind to try it again, and in that frame of mind he went his way, following his wife. Upon reaching home he found the woman in the same down cast look. When the sun was going down he called her to come forth to see the beautiful sun, she obeyed and came forth; side by side they stood gazing upon the sun that was going down. Immediately seven little children came and stood in front of them looking into the woman's face saying, "We are in hunger and the night will soon come; where is the food?" Upon hearing this, water came from the woman's eyes seven drops came and dropped upon the earth. The man reached forth his right hand and wiped away the tears from the woman's brow. It moved him so much

that his hand shook, seeing this the woman said to the
little ones, "hold your peace little ones, in seven
moons you shall be filled and shall hunger no more."
With glad hearts the children departed and were seen
no more.   On seeing this the strong man's heart was
moved and immediately he asked his wife if she would
tell him what he could do to make her happy.   She
answered and said that if he would show love to her
that would last while the world stands she would then
be happy, not only would she be happy but the whole
world be happy.   The man answered that he had
shown all the love that was in him and if she knew
any more love that he could show to tell him, and he
would show it in a manner to please her.   She
answered, that she wanted him to show such a love
that all the people might also love her, and that she
wanted a love that would last always.   The man then
said, if it is in my power to bring this about it shall
be done.   This answer brought brightness to her brow,
then turning to the man and casting her eyes fully
upon his, said with happiness, "My eyes can meet
yours, and before the sun goes down seven times, it
must then be the beginning of happiness the world
over ; and man, if you are ready to hear my request
and if you are ready to grant it, I will now make it
known."   The man answered as before saying, "If it is
in my power your request shall be granted."   Then the
woman turned her pleading eyes to him saying, "Take
the stone implement, with it slay me unto death," and
the man said, "This is beyond my power, and further it
is only the beast that slays mankind, but before the sun

goes down seven times I shall answer you." And
before the sun arose the man was on his way to the
north land to consult Klose-kur-beh upon the matter,
and when the sun was rising on the seventh day he
returned.

Klose-kur-beh had told him that her request must be
granted, because she came to the world for good, and
that none could be realized until she had fulfilled her
mission.   When this was made known to her, her joy
was great, and she gave directions as to what should be
done.   She told the man after he had slain her, to get
twisted branches of the small trees and tie the branches
around her neck and drag her body to a large open
space of land and to drag it all over the open space,
and when the flesh was worn away to the bones turn it
and wear away the other side, and after he had dragged
her body all over the land to bury her bones in the
middle of it and then come away, and in seven moons
to go and gather all he found on the land,—gather and
eat, but not all of it—save some to put in the land
again.   Let seven moons pass before you put my flesh
in the ground again; put it under the ground so the
birds will not devour it.   My bones you can not eat,
but you can burn it, and it will bring peace to you
and unto your children.   On the morrow when the sun
was rising the man did slay the woman and he dragged
her body over a large open land and did bury her bones
in the center of it as directed.   The man did not visit
the place until after the seven moons had passed, but
others went before the time came and brought from the
land long green blades of the plant which the man rec-

ognized as the same kind of blade that he saw trailing behind the woman's feet when fording the river. When the seven moons had passed the man went to the place where his wife's bones lay and when he came to the place he beheld the place filled with tall plants but not green because the sun had faded them to a yellow shade, and upon examining the stock found substance in them which he tasted and it was sweet, and he called it "Skar-moo-nal"—Corn, and upon reaching the place where the bones lay he found a plant, large, with broad leaves, without substance ; because it was bitter in taste he called it "Ootar-Mur-wa-yeh."—Tobacco. Upon his return to the people and made known what he had found there was great rejoicing among them and all went to help the man in the harvest; all the corn and tobacco were properly taken care of. And here corn and tobacco raising began.

The man whose heart had been so heavy with sorrow since slaying his wife, began to be cheerful when seeing such a general rejoicing and happiness so universal. He began to see that granting the request of his wife was for the good of all, and he no longer lay sorrow to his heart. The only perplexity to him was how to dispose of the fruits of the great event. He saw that something must be done and that in the future some wholesome management would be needed. As he was not able to come to a just conclusion of it, he called together seven young maidens and sent them to the north part of the country to get Klose-kur-beh to come among them and tell them what to do with the harvest, which was then in the peoples hands. When

the seven maidens came forth he charged them with the
mission and on the morrow, at the rising of the sun,
the young maidens did start on their journey saying
that the seven times seventh sun would bring them
back and when the shadows began to appear toward
the setting of the sun, gather themselves together
and await their coming. And when the time arrived,
which was appointed by the young maidens, all the
people gathered to welcome them home, and when the
sun began to cast its shadows toward the setting of the
sun the maidens appeared and said, Klose-kur-beh will
come immediately." When the sun was highest,
Klose-kur-beh came and immediately the people began
to show him the harvest. Upon seeing the great
store before him Klose-kur-beh showed signs of
joy and said, "There was one thing the Great Spirit
did not mention to me, therefore we must be careful in
our minds what we do with it. And because this has
come from the good of a woman's heart I must first
give thanks to the Great Spirit in the name of the
seven young maidens who brought the message to me;
and immediately he went back to the spot where he
first came that noon, and looking up to the sun did
give thanks to the Great Spirit, seven times—once for
each maiden, and then he began to speak to the people,
saying : The first words of the first mother, have come to
pass. When she first came she claimed her origin
from the beautiful blade of the plant and that her
power shall be great and it shall be felt all over the
world ; that she was all love,—even the beast will
steal her body—for the love of it. And now that she

has gone into the substance, which every living being
will love we must take care that the second seed of
the first mother be always with you, because this is
her flesh.   When you are filled with it, it gives
strength; her bones also have been left behind for
your good.   These also are the blades of the plant.
This blade will not give strength to the body, but will
give strength to the mind; burn it and inhale the
smoke it will bring freshness to the mind and your
heart will be contented while the smoke of it be in you.
These two things must always bring memory to your
minds, when you eat remember her, and do the same
when the smoke of her bones rises before you; yea
more, whatever your work be, stop in your labor until
the smoke has all gone to the Great Spirit.   And as
we are all brothers, divide among you the flesh and
bone of the first mother, and let all shares be alike,
then the love of your first mother will have been fully
carried out.

A little more I wish to say for your good.   By the
change made in your first mother, other changes in the
world shall follow.   There shall be weeping and shed-
ding of tears, and there shall be rejoicing causing the
body to move to suit the joy.   There shall be a season
to put the seed in the ground, and a season for it to
grow and then the harvest shall come.   There shall be
a season for heat and a season for cold, so prepare
yourself for all these, that when each one comes you
may be ready for it.   The end of my mission among
you has now come.   I shall leave you and shall hearken
no more to your calling, but shall wait the calling of

the Great Spirit. Strange things shall happen, but
those who bring about the changes will tell you all about
them so you may understand them. Here Klose-kur-beh
took leave of his people to come no more. Nothing
cast such a gloom over the whole country, as did the
departure of Klose-kur-beh. The first tears were then
shed among the older women. The men were silent
for a long time, and after a long continued silence the
old men began to strive to cheer up the younger. The
cause of their gloom was, that Klose-kur-beh did not
recommend any system of organization under which
the people might live.

For seven suns the people wandered aimlessly about
each day. They questioned one another as to what was
best to do. Finally it was decided that the seven
young maidens—the same who had previously been
sent after Klose-kur-beh, be called forth and point out
some method which if good, be considered by the old
men for adoption. Immediately the young maidens
were called forth and the call was obeyed and the young
maidens did make their appearance and entered the
gathering of the people which was very great.

The eldest of the maidens led the way, followed by
the others in single file. Upon entering the gathering
they all put up their hands over their eyes to hide them
when a halt was made and the leader of the maidens
then spoke these words : "In purity we seven have lived,
and in chastity must we point out to you the way we
must all live. First, we want the first Father to be
called forth so he may stand in front of us." When
the first Father had been called and was standing in

4

front of the young maidens, the leader continued her saying, calling the man ''Na-mi-ter-qui''—Father, you have
chosen us again to help you. In purity we seven have
lived, yet we are not worthy to gaze upon your brow
on this so important an occasion, therefore we have
covered our eyes. Our eyes being covered we cannot
see what is around us, yet we can see with our hidden
eyes the way which will be good for your children.

First, you shall call forth the first born seven men,
and with them you shall hold council upon all matters
and the way the people shall live. Teach them to
hearken unto the older men. This will be good, because
the more a man sees the more he knows, and a man can
learn more in two days than in one day. Therefore
heed your elders. Be very careful and have all this
done in seven moons, and in seven times seven moons
all our sayings will have been learned, then happiness will
come. Then the seven maidens bowed seven bows to the
Father and departed. All the people were well pleased
with the sayings of the young maidens and immediately
they began to look upon the Father for advice upon all
matters, and in seven moons, the seven first born men
had been consulted and the council meeting of the Red
man began.

After these regulations had been established, seven
young men were sent to cary the news to Klose-kur-
beh, and on the morrow at the rising of the sun, the
young men did start to carry the news as directed.
The young men returned saying Klose-kur-beh could not
be found. His home was standing on the same ground,
but no person in it, and no one answered their call.

The house was not empty, it is filled with the implements of stone, the number being so great that they
will last our people many times seventy years.   At
this saying the younger class of men showed more
signs of disappointment than the older ones.   They
said Klose-kur-beh had acted strangely to leave the
land without giving the power which he had to shave
out the implements of stone.   At this the Father spoke
to the young men saying that Klose-kur-beh had not
made a positive promise.   He remembered hearing him
say "that the power would be given unto them bye and
bye," therefore it will be good for us to hold our peace,
and bye and bye the power will be given unto us.   At
this the young people held their peace, and the Father
and the seven men gave directions what to be done with
the implements.   They made them last a long time, or
until the power to make more was given to the people.
Before many seven moons had passed the younger
people began to be very much discontented because
there was none among them who had the power not
only to shave out stone with wood, but likewise there
was no one that was able to talk with the animals,
trees, birds and fishes like Klose-kur-beh, and they
began to appeal to the Father and the seven men to
bring a change so that they might have some kind of
power, and they pressed their appeal so forcibly that
the old men were very much perplexed.

CHAPTER IV.

.

The winter and the seven years famine —The discovery of the first white
man's track.

Just at this period, a boy came one morning when
the sun was rising and entered the house of a man and
wife who had only one child, a son. The boy who
came. was a strange one, none could 'tell to what family
he belonged. Upon entering the house of sticks and
leaves he selected a place for himself beside the boy
of the house, who was about the same age and size as
himself. Upon being questioned whence he came and
whose son he was; and how long since he was born?
answered and said, he was the frost, the son of the air,
and that he was many times seven years old. At this
saying, the man of the house said: "Boy I do not
understand your saying. I do not know the frost,
neither do I know the time seven years; yet I know
there is a Spirit in the air." The boy answered and
said, "If you know that there is a Spirit in the air,
very well, but the frost you shall know after the
harvest has passed, after that the time shall be divided
into twelve moons, and as has been established with
you, and you are many—your moons shall be seven,
and because I am one my moons shall be five. In a
little while I shall leave you and shall talk with you
no more.—Yet you shall see me every year after your
seven moons shall have passed." And the man of
the house saw that the boy was not only a stranger,

but that he had a strange mind—a mind not the same
as the children of the people—and without further saying he let the boy remain with the boy of the house
and share his home; he took care of him in the same
manner as he did his own son, but he saw that the
strange boy di dnot grow in size like his own son.   He
began to bring his mind to the saying of the boy.
And the change he noticed was that,—there could be
seen, birds in large numbers all going toward the noon
when the seven moons had passed—After five moons
the birds would return. · Few birds remained all the
time and these were birds that could fly but a short
distance.   He also found at this time that some of the
fresh water animals built houses beside the rivers and
that they would stay in them five moons.   The larger
animals sought caves wherein they could stay during
the passing of the five moons.   No other change could
he see did these events bring about.   But when the
seven years had passed, there was a great commotion
among the people, more so among the mothers' of
little children, because a child had been found dead in
its bed, and none knew the cause of it; no mark of
violence could be found upon the body, that could
have caused death, only that its mouth was filled with
blood.   This visitation caused great excitement
because it was the first death that have come among
them.   No death ever occured only when some one
was killed and devoured by the animals.   People came
from afar off to see the dead child.   The old men were
called together to give their opinion, but none were
able to solve the mystery.   The first Father and the

seven men were called upon to direct how to dispose of
the dead body.   The men gave directions that the
body be buried deep in the ground saying, if it be
laid away for keeping, animals would come and devour
it, and if put into the water the fishes would do the
same.   This saying brought peace in all minds and the
dead body was buried deep.   The man that had charge
of the strange boy, noticed that the child acted very
strangely, during the day, he showed signs of being
sleepy and fell asleep during the day, a thing he never
did before.   This caused the man to have a suspicion
of the boy as being the one which caused the death of
the child.   So when night came, the man lay awake
watching the movements of the boy, and during his
watching he did not see the boy go out, but when the
night had been half gone the boy came in from out side
and immediately began to spread the coals of the fire
which had not gone out, and after spreading the coals
with the fire-stick, took out some substance from his
bosom and carefully laid it on the coals; and after it
had been cooked took it off and began to eat.   At this
moment the man arose and asked the boy what he was
doing? and the boy answered and said he was eating,
and the man asked him what he was eating, to which
the boy answered, "I am only eating this small tongue
of a child" at the same time offering the man a piece to
eat, which the man refused to touch, and after eating,
the boy went to bed and was soon in a deep sleep.

And when the morrow came, when the sun was
rising, another excitement came and it was greater than
the first, because another child had died the same way

as the first, and in a very short time the gathering of the people was great, because those who had come from afar to see the first child were yet in the place.

When the man of the house saw how large the gathering was, and while the strange boy was yet asleep, he went forth and told the people that it was the work of the strange boy. After the man had told what he had seen the boy do, he told the people to go and examine the dead child's mouth, and if they found his tongue gone, surely it was the boy's work whom he had seen cooked and eaten it.

Upon examining the dead body it was found that its tongue was gone, nothing in the mouth but blood. It was evident who committed the awful deed, and immediately "not only the seven" but all of the old men were called together to consult as to what should be done. While yet it was early in the day a decision had been reached and rendered to the effect, that the boy be immediately slain by the father of the one whose death the strange boy had caused first—and the second bereaved father shall help the first in binding the body of the slain with cords of strong bark, and fasten rocks to the body so it will sink, and put it into deep water where no eye can reach it that it be devoured by the fish. The two bereaved fathers after slaying the boy did cast its body into the deep water.

And when night came, before the first half had passed, while yet the fire in the house burning brightly, the same boy came in trembling, and seeing the man yet awake said, "I am cold" and he began to warm himself. After warming himself awhile, he took the

fire stick and began to spread the coals, and he took
from his bosom two tongues which he cooked as before,
and after eating them went to sleep as usual. Early on
the following morning the loud voices of men were
heard, and immediately two men rushed into the house
where the boy lay asleep, and the two men aroused
him from his slumber, and charged the boy with the
death of their two children. Seeing this the man of
the house told the men to hold their peace until the old
men had met whose directions the people must follow.
Hearing this, the two men departed in great anger,
leaving the boy to sleep again.

Early in the day the old men met, and directed the
second bereaved father to slay the boy in the presence
of all the people, and the last bereaved fathers to burn
the body to ashes, after which the four bereaved
mothers shall cast the ashes to the four winds. The
first to cast the ashes to the rising of the sun, the
second bereaved to the setting of the sun, the third to
the noon, and the fourth towards the north land.

While yet the boy was in his sleep the four men went
forth and took the boy from his bed and carried him to
a high land where the people had already gathered,
and the men slew the boy, and the other two fathers
burnt up the body to ashes, and the four mothers cast
the ashes to the four winds.

When the night came, and before the man of the
house had retired to rest, and while yet the woman was
up, the slain boy came in, his face flushed with anger,
and immediately he began to cook three tongues in the
fire, which he devoured ravenously, after which he

threw his body violently on the bed and immediately went to sleep, while the woman wrung her hands wailing with a loud moan.   Just after the first half of the night had passed, it was discovered that three children had died in the same way as the other four, and immediately there arose loud screeches of the mothers whose children laid dead in their homes, and also the tramping of many feet following the mothers who were running aimlessly about as if crazed, and the husbands of the mothers rushed to the house where the boy was sleeping to take him by force, but the man of the house advised them to leave the matter with the old men, but the fathers would not be quieted until the woman of the house spoke unto them saying, ''Hold your peace men, until after the coming of the light of day, when all the mothers shall have been awakened.   As I am a mother of a child, I know the value and the amount of love a mother holds for her child; therefore let the mothers have a voice in the matter that this cruelty may be stopped, after which we may live in peace and bring peace to our little ones.''   Hearing this the angry fathers departed in silence while yet a great uproar being heard in every direction, which was kept up until the coming of the day.   And when the sun arose the great noise went down and quietness reigned until the sun began to throw its shadows toward the setting sun and the seven first-born men got together. They sent for all the men women and children to assemble and find a way for the safety of the children. In this assemblage it was thought best to pursue peaceful measures; and a large collection of valuables

were got and put into the hands of the seven bereaved
mothers, to be presented to the strange boy, with an
earnest appeal to him to cease causing the death of
children.

The seven mothers went and laid valuables consisting
of some fine clothing of fur, the best of the stone
implements, hooks and lines, a nice bow and arrow,
also a nice canoe before the boy, begging him to desist
from further destruction of the children.   When the
boy saw what was being done by the mothers he was
very much moved, and said he was sorry for what he
had done.   Yet it was done for the people's good ; upon
speaking further he said, I have come among you when
I was many times seven years old, and I have been
among you seven years, and in all these years no notice
has been taken of me, and to call your minds to me I
have been obliged to awaken you by striking a blow
where it will be most felt.   Knowing that the mother's
heart is all to her babe, and toward that babe all
tenderness must be shown, so by striking down the
babe, the mother's spirit is quickly awakened, and soon
she wished to know the way to save her other children.

I did not come for your valuable goods, take them
back to your homes and divide them among yourselves,
because I will hearken unto your prayers without them,
and I shall grant all your requests.   But you must also
tell your people that I have requests which I ask them
to grant.   First, they must forget my works or what I
have done in the past, because what I did was necessary
for me to do.   I did this to show you how cruel I will
be, if you do not prepare yourselves to meet me when

I come in my true state and nature. You have been born and lived. No death has come since the world began, only when a beast slays you. But after my coming in my true state and nature, death by sickness will come upon you, because when I come you shall call me "Pa-poon," winter. If you are not prepared to keep your body warm with clothing, you shall be found dead with cold; but if you are not dead, you shall be taken sick and die, I shall have pity upon no one, as as there is no pity in me, I have shown it to you in taking the lives of your seven little ones. So prepare yourselves in everything for the five moons which I claim.

As sickness must come, I have brought medicine for all kinds of sickness, which I shall leave with you. Now I want you to grant this request. Before giving you the medicine for sickness, I want to have a rest, I want seven young maidens to attend me during my rest, each maiden shall attend me one year, or what you call twelve "moons" and at the end of seven years, all the seven maidens will come together and turn my body so I may lay on the other side of my body for another seven years. In turning my body in the first seven years, you shall find where my body laid, seven sprouts of plants starting from the ground; let them grow seven moons, when the young maidens shall name what disease each plant shall cure; then they shall gather the seed from them and shall scatter it to the four winds, as you did my ashes, and the seed shall grow all over the land, and it will be the medicine for the sick. After this is done the young maidens shall have finished their part. Then the duty of the young men shall begin. While I was with my father, the air, I heard the wailing of your young men because no power have been given them to shave out implements from the stone; I have come to give that as well as medicine for sickness. But first, when the young maidens have finished their work, a seven times seven young men who having no wives, shall attend me, seven shall attend me one year, then another seven for another year, and such change shall take place among them every year until the seven years have ended; There must be one awake from among them all the time; if at any time all go asleep and none to watch me I shall arise and leave them, and all that I am to give shall be lost.

But if they heed my saying and watch faithfully, when the end of the seven years have come, all of the seven times seven shall assemble in my presence and shall stay with me the last seven times seven nights and days, who shall go fasting and shall eat once in every seven days and nights. But none shall go asleep during the passing of the seven times seven nights and days. There shall be no power given to those that are found asleep at the end of that time.

As I have come to do good I shall ask nothing only what the young men can do, therefore I say that when the time comes for the seven young men's turn to watch, all may go asleep but one, whose eyes shall be on me one day and one night, when another takes his place for the next night and day.

Once in seven days and nights the young man shall take his turn in watching over me.

As I have come to bring medicine to you which you shall give to those who shall become sick, I also bring death, and those that are too much exposed to my nature shall die.

After the young maidens have finished their work and the young men have commenced on their part, the spirit in me shall become changed, because I am to give the spiritual power, therefore none shall touch my body; and one heeds not my warning and touches me shall drop and die.

And as I have been distructive to your children, and that same destructive power still remain in me, you must be very careful in keeping the little ones away from the range of my eyes, because when a little one comes within seven times seven paces and my eyes fall fully on them they shall fall and die. And for your safety and your childrens safety I shall now take out all the bones of my body leaving only enough in me so that when the two seven years have ended I can take them back into my body, also there may be something come that will require the use of what have been left in me. But be very careful in putting away beyond my reach those bones I have been taking out, because if you leave them near me I will reach forth and put back all you have put away and shall be able to depart without you knowing and not receive the good I am to give. In taking the bones out of my body, will show you two things; First, that when there are no bones in the body it will not be able to move. The second thing shown, will be the greatness of the power in the air.

It is the air that have sent me, because I am the son of the air, and before I leave you, you shall have been given the greatest power the man will ever have, and on the last day I will give the young men all the instruction how to use and how to retain it." Having ended his saying, the boy reached forth his right hand and began to take the bones out of his right foot and leg, then out of the left foot and leg, hand and arm, also the ribs on both sides of the body leaving only the back-bone and the bones of the head, also the right hand and arm. And the seven maidens who had already been selected, did put away the bones out of his reach, and then laid the body on its left side where it is to lay, and did lay, to the end of the seven years. After the boy's body had been laid in its proper place he said,"After this you shall call me "No-chi-gar-neh"— bone handler." And the faithful maidens did their duty to the satisfaction of the boy and to the joy of the old people.

Having performed all the duties required of them, the young maidens went through the task of turning the body of No-chi-gar-neh, and in doing so did see the seven plants coming through the ground in the place where the boy's body had been laying which they left to grow. And when the seven moons have passed and after gathering the seed and having named each plant and what disease they will cure, did cast the seed in the four winds, which ended the works of the seven maidens.

And after the maidens had departed the seven times seven young men took their turn in the watching. They asked the old men to divide them into sevens, and

to select the first seven who are to do the caring
and watching the first year, and also those who shall do
that duty the next year.   And the old men did divide
them into sevens and assigned each their year of duty.
When the first seven began on their task they found
No-chi-gar-neh restless and breathing heavy, but dare
not touch his body because they had been forbidden
to do so.   But when the first seven days have passed,
he became more quiet so that he closed his eyes and
begun to gaze steadily out in the open space in front of
the house.   And it happened at that moment a child
crossed the space in the range of his gaze immediately
fell dead.   And the old men went to him and told him
what had happened, the news of which moved him
very much, and he said to them, "I have warned you
of this, but children will be children, therefore something must be done and for the sake of the little ones,
before the sun goes down I shall close my eyes, but
first all the seven times seven young men shall get
together so they be present and see it done."   And
after the young men had assembled No-chi-gar-neh
lifted up his right hand to his eyelids and drew them
one by one down to the lower part of his face where
they remained in the position as they had been drawn.
After this had been done he said, "There will be no
more trouble with the little ones," bade the young men
to depart in peace, which the young men obeyed
leaving only those who were on duty to remain.   No
more trouble took place so that a good care could be
given to No-chi-gar-neh.

When the allotted time had arrived all the young
men assembled to watch and to fast in the seven times

seven days and nights. This proved an arduous duty to
perform ; so much so that when the end of time had come
only seven were found awake, the rest having gone to
sleep. And when No-chi-gar-neh was told that only
seven of the young men were awake and the rest were
in sleep, he said, "Seven is a true number, I am glad in
my heart that the nature has made a good selection,
therefore let all the seven times seven young men have
seven days' and seven nights' rest, and on the seventh
day send back to me the seven young men that are
now awake. Let no others come, and when all the
young men have gone home to rest, let the seven old
men come before me because I have much to say
concerning the people. Let the seven young men who
are not in sleep wake those that are in sleep so that
they may all go their way, for I have nothing to say to
the ones that are in sleep," And as soon as No-chi-gar-
neh finished his talk the seven young men did wake all
those that were in sleep and all went their way, each one
to his home.

And when the sun was in the noon the old men
entered the house where No-chi-gar-neh was laying,
and after he was told that the old men had come he
said to them, "Only seven days and seven nights longer
I am to be with you in the same flesh as your flesh, as
after that time has passed I will come in a different
substance once in every seven moons and you will not
see me as you do now, you shall only feel the presence
of my spirit, a spirit which will not give comfort to you
nor to your children, and this shall be so while the
world stands. Because in happiness you came into the
world, but in sorrow you shall live in it, for I shall

bring sorrow unto those that are not prepared for my coming because when I begin to come you shall reckon your time by years as there shall be winters and summers."

Here No-chi-gar-neh commanded the oldest man to tell him when his right hand was toward the noon sun, as he could not see because his eyelids were drawn down. He lifted up his right hand in a circular manner, and when it was toward the sun, the old man told him it was toward the sun.

There, he said: My hand now points to the sun; The sun is the summer. When he comes near I will go away, for he will have no pity for me, he will melt my white robe in which I come and I shall go away without it, but I shall return with another the next year.

When the seven days rest had ended and the seven young men having returned to him, he said to them, let no man be near me and you when the sun is down, because when night has come you will know no one, you will be restless, yet you will not know it because you will be in a trance ready to receive the spiritual power I am going to bring upon you; be not afraid nothing will befall you while in that state.

By the order of nature I was in the trance while the first seven days and nights was passing, yet I am here ready to set back my bones, and after that and while you will be in the trance, I will draw back my eyelids to where they belong, and I will then be ready to do my work. In bringing the spiritual power upon you, ask no question for I will answer none. My work to

6

me is plain. But although you will have the power
that others do not possess, yet it will be always a
mystery to you how it comes to those that possess it,
because none is awake when the Spirit enters, it enters
while the person sleeps; therefore the spirit of sleep
will tell you what to do. There will be many who are
filled with the false spirit, but the spirit that is coming
to you will be the true one, and it will only go from
you to your children, none others will be able to get it
because none were awake when the time came to
receive it.

I will take you up far above the ground where the current of the air is pure, and in the midst of the spiritual
body of the air, and where the current conveys the
spirit of the air from all quarters of the land, there you
shall be filled with the spirit. And after being filled
you shall have the power so you shall be able to shave
out stone to any shape and form you want with the
fragments of the wood from the tree that has been
shattered by the ball of fire that shot from the clouds.
You shall also have the power so you can turn yourselves into anything you wish that has the spirit in it;
you will be able to travel in the air, in the water and
under the water; you shall be able to talk with not
only the spirit of the animals, but with the animals
themselves. Birds and fishes you shall talk with.
Your power shall be according to the amount of your
faith; he that believes in the spirit shall be filled with
the spirit, and his power shall be great; and he that
believes not in the spirit shall have power only according to the strength of his body. All of you shall be

filled with the spirit before the sun rises again ; and
being filled, your power shall be great, yet you shall not
have the power to give it to another because such
power shall come to those only who are chosen by the
spirit of the air.

Having been chosen by your fathers to be among the
seven times seven, and moreover, having been selected
by the spirit of the air to be the seven who shall
receive this great power, it is proper for me to say that
when the next sun shines on your faces you shall be
great men among your people, because your works shall
bring great comfort to yourselves also to all your people,
for you shall be useful to them. Having no power to
give to others the same as you possess, yet you shall be
able to take the strength away from your brother who
shall remain weak for a while. This power shall come
to you to show how much the spirit of the air is able to
do for a man, so that all may believe in the spirit and
in you.

Being great, great must be your care in keeping
yourselves in this greatness. You must never allow
yourselves to become so small as to use your power upon or against your brother on any contention. Do not
abuse one another with this power.

"When you have so far forgotten my saying and
begin to use this power against your brother, then the
time is near when it shall depart from you, because
whoever abuses this power shall lose it. Oh, would
that your minds be equal to the great lesson which this
mysterious power and privilege will enforce upon them
you would become a great people, because all the arts

man must have are embodied in these many mysterious
powers which are good food for study ; therefore should
you let them pass by unobserved, then misfortune will
follow, because you will have lost all the power and
arts it would have produced and it shall never return,
because all shall return to the spirit of the air. Above
all things, you seven that the power be given must
never abuse one another with it, and you must teach
those who will be fortunate enough to get the same
power never to abuse it. Teach them also never to
abuse the spirit of the animals. You may kill the
animal and eat his flesh but never abuse the spirit of
it, because if you do abuse the spirit of the animal he
will never come to your calling. In calling to you the
spirit of any thing, you shall not call it into your house
with your family, but you shall build one for the purpose which must be made strong because many will
come in a rough manner and shake the house for each
shall want to show man the power the spirit has.

Now that the time has come and the people are in
their sleep, I will call forth the oldest of your seven to
come to me now. And when the young man obeyed
and had advanced to the side of the boy ; the boy said,
now all may arise and listen to my words ; to which all
the young men obeyed and when standing by his side,
he said to them, my bones are with us but are laying
beyond my reach, twice seven years have they been
laying where your people have placed them, and as I
have no more work to do for you as the spirit of the
air will this night do its own work.

As I am the son of that spirit, when you bring my
bones the touch of them will have much effect upon

you, it will so effect you, you will know no one and you will not know one another, you will have no thought nor feeling, yet you will all realize what is passing around you during the coming of the spirit. Up high in the air you shall receive it. And after the spirit have come in you, you shall see many things which others who are without this spirit do not see.

The things you will see you will never forget. The time surely has now come, and only a few more words then all shall be done. For fear the people may doubt my works, it will be necessary for you to show them the power you get this night, so when you have come down from the air each one of you shall go to your home, and on the morrow when the sun is highest you shall all meet on a high ground and there build a house the entrance of which shall be low, so that you creep like the babe in entering it ; but the top shall be made open. The house shall be low but very strong. Seven days you shall be in building it, and on the seventh day at noon all of you shall enter and close the door so that no other shall enter with you. After this is done, one of you, he that entered first shall sing, and in his singing shall call the spirit of every living thing, and the different spirits will come to the call. And after you have talked with them they shall all depart, and you shall then come out of the house and take it all apart so it shall not stand there to be put to other use. After you have gone through all this, you shall then have done your part and shall go home to stay. You the eldest of the seven, go forth and bring to me the bones of my left arm, and the others bring the other bones.

And the eldest obeyed and brought forth the bones No-chi-gar-neh called for.

Upon laying his hand on the bones, the young man began to tremble and shook violently so that he went into a trance, and when the others laid their hands on the bones to bring to the boy it effected them the same way. Thus the seven were in a trance and did not realize the presence of each other. Yet each one had a vision; the memory of which lasted during all their lives. All did realize that they were high up in the air so that they could see the whole world and the face of it, could see all that was moving and could hear all the sounds of the world as the face of the earth was like the smooth ice so that nothing was hid from their eyes. But upon looking in the direction where the sun rises there was a thick vapor standing in the middle of the ocean beyond which they could see nothing, yet they could hear sounds like those made by man. And upon looking around they saw that No-chi-gar-neh was not with them, he had departed to come no more. And they began to come down,— and soon were all on the earth, and when the sun arose all went their way each one to his home.

And when the noon came, the seven did meet on a high ground as commanded by No-chi-gar-neh, and did build the house as they had been directed; and when it was built and ready to be entered, all the people came to witness the calling of the spirits; many came from afar off, so that a very large crowd of people surrounded the house, but none were allowed to enter with the spiritual men. And after closing the door, and when the singing begun, the house shook, and when a spirit arrived the whole people could hear its arrival because it shook the house violently, and the people did hear all what the spirits said to the men in the house, but could see nothing come nor anything depart. After the spiritual conferences had ended, and the spiritual men got out, they did take the house all down and apart, and each one was allowed to rest from all social intercourse for seven days, and after the seven days had passed the old men began to visit them separately to learn from them all they saw while being filled with the spirit. This the young men found to require a long time to accomplish as the old men were obliged to go through the examination by making inquiries of them separately and then compare the reports from them so that all things be learned as in one mind.

After this was done, then the old men began to teach all the people what had been done and what the people ought to do. The first change that could be seen to take place after the people had witnessed what had been transpiring, was that many of them were taken the idea of singing. First, after the manner as in calling the spirit, but after a long while they sung all kind of ways, each singer composed its own music, but when one composed music that suited the people it would be learned and sung by many other singers. No written music was ever gotten up, neither were the words ever composed for any music, therefore there were no songs with words which the people could learn and sing. True, there were in some instances words repeated in the singing, but never more than four or five words, only enough to

indicate what prompted the singer to sing.   The next change
and the most remarkable one that followed, was the idea of
reckoning of time from the moons to years.

This the people looked upon as most important because
in seven years the winter was to come and it seemed that
the people were almost at a loss, hardly a score of them
could agree upon any given time.   At all events, the seven
years waiting was a long one, and many changes came
before the winter made its appearance.   When the old men
began to teach the young, it was necessary for them to reckon
the time in their teaching by the generations, because every
old generation must teach the younger, of things that have
passed.

After getting ready for the winter many times, but it
came not, the people were much puzzled, and in their perplexity their minds were very much diversified in the matter of
reckoning.   Some claimed that seventy times seven moons
had passed, while others say seven hundred have gone by;
some say only seven years, while the old teachers claimed
that seven generations have come since No-chi-gar-neh left
them.   The reckoning of the teachers had more weight
among the people than the others on account of the
increased state of the population since No-chi-gar-neh went
away.   But the old teachers themselves were very much
bewildered because the winter had not come; and having
been so much said about it, the attention of the young
people was called to it, and after the young people had
much talk, reminded the old folks of their teaching.   They
said that they had been taught that when winter was near

all plants shall be changed from green colors to grey and
the leaves fall off the trees. This reminder of the young
folks opened the eyes of the old, so nothing more was said
or done only to watch the appearance of the plants and
leaves.

In about seven moons the whole land began to change ;—
air cold, cold winds began to blow, and nights chilly, and
finally frost and ice was found in places some mornings.
Birds began to gather in flocks and flew away toward the
noon. At last the snow began to fall which covered the
whole land, and the old men called it "Pa-poon," winter.
There has been so much said about the coming of winter,
and the people were so well prepared for it, none perished by
the cold, but many made sick by undergoing the long
exposure, but these were soon made comfortable by the
mothers who took care the medicinal plants that had been
gathered by the maidens previous to the changing of the
color of the plants. The gathering of the medicinal plants
and putting them in the care of the mothers made the people
look upon them as the healers of the sick, who when called
upon went to their work with willing hands, so that when the
winter had rolled by only seven deaths were reported, while
seven times that many had been relieved. Thus having
conducted the medical department so faithfully and well, the
duty of dealing out medicine fell to the women, therefore
there was no man doctor among them. This arrangement
continued until after the coming of the white man. To deal
out medicine to the sick was looked upon as below the sphere
of man ; surgical profession was not known and the practice

of surgery was not needed, because those who dealt out
medicine were able to heal all kinds of diseases, bones and
flesh were healed alike.   Men's minds were entirely absorbed
in the art of spiritual works.   A good hunter was also
considered useful, more so when the country became more
thickly populated.

But the spiritual men were considered indispensible beings.
No matter how great a hunter a man may be, he is bound to
consult these men upon all occassions, therefore the services
of them were constantly sought after and were always busy.

The people having multiplied to such an extent that about
all of the stone implements made by Klose-kur-beh had been
divided up amomg them, and when more were needed the
spiritual men were called upon to make them.

When winter came and the snow got deep, the hunters
were sore with trouble not knowing how to get around to
their hunting in such a deep snow.

One day some boys came out to play in the snow and in
their sports made themselves some foot wear out of some
bended branches of trees which they filled the middle part
with the strips of bark of the "Wicki-bi-mi-si," Bass wood,
having filled the middle part and had fastened the shoes to
their feet was able to travel about on top of the snow.   The
old men seeing this done, the idea of making snow shoes soon
prevailed all over the country, and as the use of them gave so
much satisfaction that the filling of them was considered too
weak, and a more substantial substance was sought, and strips
of green hide was applied to satisfaction, and this substitute
in place of Wicki-bi-mi-si, having been put into them, the

old men called them "Unk-mock,"—snow shoes. Having
invented the snow shoes, the hunters were able to travel the
country at will, seeking game. The game was so plentiful
the people did not suffer much in want of it. There was
such a supply of game meat with the corn that was saved in
the harvest, made the people happy during the winter.
These winters came regularly just as No-chi-gar-neh had told
them, so preparations were always made to meet them. As
the winters came one after another, the people got more used
to them and the death roll became less, that is according to
the population. Therefore the people increased in numbers
very much.

The people were contented and lived like so many brothers,
everything seemed to be within their reach, a want was not
known among them until after many times seventy generations
had come, when a spirit of May-May came to a noted
spiritual man. The May-May came to tell the man
of the seven years of plenty to be followed by a seven years
of famine, which will bring much suffering, because there
shall come snow and hail which will cover all the land in
great depths, and the May-May warn them to prepare for
the coming event.

Knowing that the May-May had proved himself to be a
true friend to man in the beginning of the world, the people
were ready to heed his warning. Corn was planted,
harvested and stored in the log cribs, more than ever
before and guarded against waste, until the seven years of
plenty had passed when the seven years of famine was
expected to begin.

None knew how it was to come, but when the summer had passed and winter came, it came in a fury, the snow fell in great depths which continued for seven days when a heavy hail storm followed for the same length of time, and then on the top of these came a cold rain which lasted seven more days, then came the severe cold seven moons which froze the wet snow and hail solid like the rock, the old men called it "Po-quar-mi," —ice.

The description of the condition of the people during the coming of the ice on the earth never has been told to the traditional story tellers, therefore this part will have to be omitted. This much however was gathered; that after the big storm and when the severe and intense cold had lasted seven moons with no signs of melting, all hopes of seeing the summer to return was abandoned, and the planting of corn likely to be dispensed with for the next seven years, also the outlook for the yearly harvest of "Pun-nuk,"--ground nuts, or the wild potatoes, so disappointing that the people began to look forward to find some substitute to take place of the food that had been kept back by the long snow and ice weather.

At last the people were obliged to send out men of good judgment to seek game for the whole people, a game that can be easily obtained whether it be big or small; anything that will do for food.

These men soon returned who reported that enough game had been found to supply all the people and had brought some home with them, consisting of small animals and birds, which the old men called "Mar-ta-qua-so,"—Rabbit, and

"Pus-keh-gur-targi-leh,"—Spruce Partridge. The men found the country full of such food game.

Their report upon the discovery of the larger game yet existing wiped away the fear into which the people had been thrown, who feared that the deep snow and ice had lain so long on the earth had destroyed many living things, therefore these happy tidings filled the people with much joy, although the men say that the large game could not be got, as the smoothness of the country with the hard ice enables them to get easily out of man's reach. But the mere knowledge of the animals surviving the destructive period then passing, was enough to create a general rejoicing.

When the people went after the food game which had been discovered, they found the birds in the bog lands feeding on the boughs of the short and scrubby bog spruces, and found the bogs filled with them, and were so tame that the person wishing to gather a supply, could, without difficulty, knock them off and down from the trees. But after a while they found that this process soon disturbed the tameness of the birds and a commotion showed itself among them at the coming of the man.

And when the people discovered this, a method of snaring them was adopted which proved to be the thing desired. The method of securing the right kind of material to make the snares was soon found by pounding out the grains of the "Arlik-ba-ter-her,"—brown ash, and splitting it into strings was just the thing wanted. And out of these ash strips made the snares which they fastened to the end of a long pole with which they could easily snare the birds by passing the loop over their heads and could draw them down without disturbing the rest of the birds. These birds were always found in a flock so large that the people moved their families to them from which they could secure food for their families for many moons. The rabbits were also found in large numbers who haunted the land between the bogs and the hard and higher lands. These were also caught with the snares made from the strips of the bark of "Wik-ki-bi-mi-si," bass wood. The snares were placed in such a manner in the rabbits path that the little animal put its head into it while passing along, but the size of the open space left in the snare would not admit the body, therefore the noose tightens around its neck and the animal gets strangled.

After the snow and ice period had passed, the spruce patridge and the rabbit were the principal winter food for those less able to go on long journeys for larger game, therefore this kind of game was afterwards reserved for the old and infirm. No able bodied man was allowed to take much of it, none seemed to care to interfere with it because everybody had been instructed from childhood to help and provide for the old and infirm, consequently this protective practice was kept up until the white man came.

CHAPTER V.

The fish famine—The capture of the white swan and the white spiritual men driven away.

The people in those days were so interested in these poor and unfortunate ones, that men would go and build winter wigwams and move them near those bogs from which they could secure their daily food.

After the food game had been found the people became more contented, and with a composure waited for the summer to come. During the snow and ice period no sickness or death was reported and the good health seemed to prevail among all, until the hot weather came, when some were taken with the bad cough, in some cases death was the result, because the medicine could not be properly administered to all. Before the winter came to a close, some of the people who were less favored with the natural patience got very much discontented notwithstanding the new discovery made, but had gone around to agitate a spirit among the people for a southern exodus. And by going around among the several tribes or bands got quite a following, and many families did start to seek summer in the south, and although the summer did return in due season, but did not bring back the families that went out to seek it, nor have they returned to this day. Their departure somewhat cast a gloom over the land. None of the old men would go, they warned those that were so ready to go of the danger of their light and inconsiderate disposition and habits, telling them that a time is coming when a man be reckoned according to his mind and habits, and if he be so that he is not contented and will not stay where the Great Spirit has placed him, but sets himself adrift, knowing not where he shall land, shall some day wish to stay to a place where he cannot, because having started himself on a drift, drifting about he must become and continue in it. But no argument could change their minds and they started for the south.

Nothing more can be said than that the people were now anxiously waiting for the coming of summer. Just about this time the May-May appeared again ; this time he came in a very happy manner, his coming was known by his happy singing while yet he was a long way off. And when near enough, and had alighted said, "not in in the spirit, but in the flesh," and with gladness I have come, and I sing with joy, not because this being my last visit to you, no ; I sing because the summer is coming. In seven moons with the help of the warm wind from the noon, the sun will melt the ice away. In seven suns hence, a natural snow will fall and it shall be seven hands deep, but the sun will melt it all away in seven days, and in melting it, will effect the ice which now covers the land, so that in seven moons all will be gone. I sing because nothing like this will befall you again while the world stands. After delivering his message May-May departed to come no more. And when the seven suns had passed, a snow fell which covered the ground seven days, and during these seven days some young men were out on a hunt, and accord-

ing to custom had taken one old man with them, and
on coming out to the seashore in a little cove where a
small brook came out to the sea, the young men discovered a man's track upon the high land, the track
begun from the shore and back to it, and around the
brook of the fresh water, which appeared to them that
some one had been carrying water from the brook to
the salt water shore, but no canoe of any kind could
be seen moving as far as they could see. When this
news was brought to the old man he at once proposed
to investigate the matter, so all hands went down, and
upon comparing the strange tracks to those they made,
there was a vast difference in three ways, first, the
person that made the strange tracks must have had on
moccasins made of hard substance ; second, the tracks
were larger than theirs ; third, and the most strange
part of all, the toes pointed outward instead of inward
like those they made themselves.

Upon arriving at a conclusion, that the tracks were
made by a strange person, it so affected the old man that
he shed tears, saying, that whoever made the tracks must
have been very lonely, and said further, that as his
strength was reduced to weakness by old age he could not
overcome the emotion that came upon him. Although
the reason the old man gave to the young men was
a good one, yet they said among themselves that something more must be the cause of the old man's weeping,
and they immediately started homeward ; and at their
arrival among their people, and reporting their discovery
and the weeping of the old man, the other old men got
together to discuss the matter and the old man who

6

had been overcome with grief was called in to explain his action while with the young men. And to the old men he said, "Upon seeing the strange tracks, all the warnings which have been given us, how that a time is coming when we must look for the coming of the white man from the direction of the rising sun, and the tracks were so very strange, not like our people's tract, came upon me so fresh I could not withhold the tears that rushed upon my brow. Knowing that a great change must follow his coming it made me weak and the weakness overcame me, because his coming will put a bar to our happiness, and our destiny will be at the mercy of the events. Being satisfied that me and the young men have seen the tracks of this strange man, it becomes as our gravest duty to prepare ourselves and people so to be ready to meet the changes which may follow." When the other old men had learned of all that had been seen, it came heavier upon them, than did the departure of Klose-kur-beh. This news was spread among all the people, even the little children were told what had been seen and what is coming to them. The commotion it created was so great that the people hardly realized that the natural snow so lately fallen was fast melting away and the ice had become like the honeycomb and must soon follow the snow. When the time came which had been set by May-May, the summer came, bringing with it the birds, leaves, plants and flowers. Corn was put into the ground which in due season came up out of the ground with all the appearance of much promise, and with a good attention and care a good crop was gathered at the harvest, which brought back the old happiness which the people enjoyed for many times seventy summers and winters, and things continued in that way until the fish famine came which was brought about in this way.

Long after the people had become great in numbers and the tribes or bands large, a very dense fog came over the whole country and remained seven moons, and during that time no fish could be found, all methods applied to get them failed, therefore the supply of food became scant because there was also considerable difficulty experienced in getting other game food owing to the density of the fog then hanging over the land. People began to be hungry, children crying for something to eat, mothers became disheartened, and the men worrying because they could not find game animals fast enough to supply their families ; and finally the people got so desperate that they began to seek the aid of the spiritual men to find the cause of all this.   To quiet the people in their fear and excitement, the most noted spiritual men, those that are in the near vicinity called other spiritual men from all parts of the country, some came from the most remote part of the land, and after getting together and selecting seven good men from among them, those seven begun to labor in their spiritual way to search and find out the cause.   In the daytime they examined the land and water, nights they arose in the air, and their seven days labor brought no fruit.

But upon their rising in the air on the seventh night, heard voices of men on the sea in the direction where the sun rises.   To this their attention was directed, but after exhausting all their power in their efforts to see the men whose voices they had heard failed and were obliged to come down, still deep in their ignorance of the cause. And after telling what they had done and the poor success they had met, the old men got together again and after much deliberation it was decided to send to north land for help. And immediately seven little girls were selected and brought together in front of the youngest ones wigwam where they repeated these words, "Oh, mother we are hungry, please bring us food." Seven times did these children repeat this and at the end of the seventh calling, "Mata-we-leh,"—loon was heard coming through the air from the north land. And after making seven circles around where the children was standing, lowered and was soon standing among the little ones, and it was here seen that instead of being a loon it was an aged woman. No one knew who she was, neither did she make herself known to the people, but in silence stood there before them facing the north land, and while thus she stood, a gentle breeze of wind came from that direction. This was pleasing to the people because no wind had swept over the land for the last seven moons, which continued until all the fog had been blown away toward the noon, leaving the land and sea clear. And as soon as the land had been cleared the woman turned her face in the direction where the sun rises, and steadily gazed upon an object which was in the mid-ocean, and without turning her face from that direction raised her left hand as if calling some one from the north land. This she repeated seven times. After she had done this she turned to the crowd of

people which was then great, and for the first time
since her arrival spoke to them and said, "The cry
of your little ones has been heard in the north land,
and I have come to their calling, and soon their little
hearts as well as all other hearts will be made glad, and
when I leave you, you shall be happy until you have fallen
into the ways of these people ;" pointing her hand toward
the mid-ocean, "who are floating there, and who have
brought upon you this trouble and hunger, you cannot
find the animals because the days have been so dark,
you cannot find fish because there is a covering over
all the fish which the power of these people have placed
there, it is the spiritual power that is in them, and if
the power that is in you has not the force to overcome
it, woe unto you." Then the woman turned to the
spiritual men who were standing near and called forth
the one nearest to her and said, "bring forth the stone,"
pointing to a very large rock which was near them,
but it was so large and heavy the man did not have the
strength to carry it and returned without it; and the
woman called the next spiritual man, who also failed to
accomplish the feat. Upon this another man was
called until the seven had been called and failed.
Then the woman went forth and took up the stone
which she carried to the edge of the sea and threw it
out in the ocean which, instead of sinking rebounded and
laid on the surface of the water. The woman then
said, "There, how can fish be seen when there is such
a covering over the water." This covering has been
placed there by the spiritual power of these men we
see in the mid-ocean. And it is my duty now either

to capture these persons or make them flee for their
safety. If we succeed in capturing them, their mission
in bringing misery and suffering among you will virtu-
ally be at an end. But if they succeed in making their
escape, look for them again some day in the same
direction. If I succeed in driving them away with the
power given me from the north land, they will learn
the power of it, and will never come again in the
spiritual form, but shall depend upon the power they
have gathered in their learning, and with such, he will
next come, and when he comes watch him closely
because by so doing you will learn the many forms of
power that is in man. After the woman had finished
saying these words, she turned to the spiritual men
and said to them, "Men come forth and bring with you
in your right hands, the fragments of wood the same
that you use when you shave the stone into implements,
and stand near the water;" and the spiritual men came
forward and took a position each one as commanded.
Then the woman said again, "Let the mothers of these
seven little girls who sent up the cry to the north land
for help, lead them to this spot that they may draw in
the "K'chi-wump-toqueh"—white swan, after I make
fast to it."

And the mothers of the seven little ones brought
their children forth as commanded. Then the woman
pulled out seven spears of long hair from her locks
which was the color of the raven, and which she
twisted into a small rope, which she placed in her left
hand and then she put her right hand into her bosom
and from under her garments pulled out a piece of

bone which was shaped like the spear, and the color of
which was red just like the blood. To this blood
colored little spear the woman fastened the hair rope,
and took the spear in her right hand, gave to the seven
little girls the other end of the hair rope to hold in
their hands, saying: "When you hear the swan cry
in pain, draw in the rope until the bird be laying at
the feet of the seven men, then your work will be
done, and let your mothers take you away in peace."

And again the woman said to the spiritual men:
"When the little girls have drawn the bird to them
and still have life in him let the oldest of you cut off
his head with the wood he holds in his hand. Then
let the next oldest cut off the right wing, and the next
man shall cut off the left wing, and the fourth man
shall cut open the birds belly, while the last three men
be standing ready to cut off the heads of the three
persons who are inside of the bird, you shall know
they are the right ones because they are white, the
same color like the bird. After cutting off their heads
let all the bodies lay near the water to be covered up
by the shaking of the water and land. It may be so
that I fail in capturing them and they escape, if so,
the little girls will only draw in a dead swan, because
the three spiritual men will have made a large hole in
its back through which they have flown. And the
swan you shall let lay to be covered up with the fragments of the earth, and the water will wash it away.
Though these men may escape the shaking of the
water and land, they may be far away when it comes,
yet they shall feel the shake of it, and shall hear the

sound, and a fear shall come upon them so they will
never come to you again with the spiritual power
because the shake of the water and the shake of the
land they shall always fear.   And it is well that there
be some power reserved which shall be brought upon
those who shall become so great in power that others
will not be able to overcome, and it is well also that,
will and might shall have a short life.   The man of
will and might shall enjoy his own way until all the
land he occupies shakes until it shall open, wherein he
shall fall, and shall not have the power to get out
because in all his works he shall never be able to find
the way to escape it."

After this saying, the woman raised up the little
spear with her right hand and threw it at the swan
which was laying in the mid-ocean, and when it was
going through the air the woman flew after it, she being
in the form of the white loon, and the people saw the
swan in its efforts to rise, but the little spear had done
its work and the bird's cry with pain was plainly
heard, and the little girls began to haul in on the rope
until the game was drawn ashore which was found
dead.   Nothing could be seen on the bird excepting
one large hole in its back.   And upon looking into
this hole only three vacant seats could be seen, and at
this moment the white loon was coming toward the
land, part of the time on the surface and another
moment be under the water.   When it came where the
body of the swan lay, and upon getting out of the
water and had transformed herself to a woman said:
"Now I shall carry back this piece of bone to the north

land and before the sun goes down I will return and
shall then break up all the covering which have been
hiding the fish; and when it breaks up, it shall fly in
pieces to the shore into piles, and whatever fragment
remains you shall keep and shall make into some useful implements, because it being the fragment of the
first contention between you and the strange people.
When the covering breaks there will be a great shock,
therefore you must all go away from this spot, go far
back on the high land, from where you can look down
and see the work." At this the woman pulled the
spear out of the dead swan's body, and the people
began to go back on to the high lands.

And after getting on to a safe place and upon looking
down to the sea, beheld the same white loon coming
from the north very swiftly, and when it reached the
place opposite where the dead swan lay, it made its
usual circles, there it stood very high and very still for
a few moments, then it turned itself into a great ball of
fire, and fell swiftly down to the water; and when it
struck the water, the earth shook and the roar of it was
great. So great was the roar, all the land shook and
stood trembling for a long time, and the commotion of
the water was also very great which brought the fishes
to the surface and could plainly be seen jumping glee-
fully out of the troubled waters. This great shock also
brought back the fog. The return of the fog, however,
was but a short duration, it only remained seven days
and when it cleared away and the sun shone there was
much happiness, because the people were already catch-
ing as many fishes as was needed.

In the midst of this happiness it was found that the woman had gone to the north land, had departed while the fog was prevailing, and upon going down to the seashore, the people found fragments of stone in large heaps all along on the shores of the coast.

Remembering what had been commanded them, they gathered the stone and made into small implements. They were not able to make the large tools out of it, because the spiritual men were not able to shave it with the wood. They could only shape it by hacking and chipping off the edges so to make small spears and arrow heads. Seeing this the old men called the stone "Keh-tungu-so-arpusque," spirit stone. The heaps of these stones remained on the shores many times seventy summers and winters, and the time it remained in these heaps the spiritual men were able to gather and save a very large amount of it for future uses; so much of it was saved that it lasted until after the white man introduced among them tools made from different substances.

In all these years while all these different events were taking place, the spiritual men were busy faithfully performing what was required of them. All were working for the good of the people, never showed among themselves any other kind of feeling only that was kind and brotherly, until after the white man was seen sailing in his strange craft along the coast.

This long looked for event created such a stir that the noted men were called to discuss the matter and to see what must be done about it, and on their getting together it was decided that there shall be some good spiritual men selected and sent on along the coast to

watch the strange people's movements. These people
were considered very strange because they were not
white as the snow, and not so white as the people
expected them to be, but were brown and hairy people.
Whether they were creatures with the speech or not,
none knew because no one had heard them talk.
However it was determined to have them watched and
this watching to continue until his true description and
habits had been learned. As has been said before
that no trouble among the spiritual men had come, but
as soon as the selection of the best and noted of them
had been made and became known, those that were
considered less noted and had not received the appoint-
ment became jealous of their brother spiritual men
who had been selected, and immediately began to show
their feeling towards them, a feeling which showed
hatred, and began to do their work in getting followers
and gathering them into their folds. And as soon as
they saw that the people were also divided in the
approval of the selection, declared themselves as enemies of the selected ones. They declared that the
people had trampled upon and had abused them,—the
same kind of power existed in them as well as in those
that had been preferred; and that the time had arrived
they must show them how much power they possessed.
And after declaring and had entered into this deter-
mination, the disappointed spiritual men began to
agitate the minds of their friends to discord, each of
them having a large influence among the people, the
whole country was thrown into different bands. Seeing this, the disappointed soon made aggressive move-

ments against the selected; although the old men advised peace and harmony, their advice was only met with scorn by the disappointed ones, saying, "That the people will never know the power that is in those that they discarded until it be shown them, and this they are bound to do." Here the intersview with them ended and the old men turned away from them with heavy hearts and great sorrow, because the happiness of the red man have now come to its end. With a depressing spirit, each old man went to his own lodge, only to point out with trembling hand to those that loves peace the destiny of the red man. When this became known the lodges of the old men were constantly thronged by the populace, not only to quiet them and reduce the sorrow they exhibited, or to alleviate the grief that was bowing down their already bent and feebled frames; but also to learn the true prophecy which was expected of them. When interviewed, they hid nothing, but were very frank in giving their views upon what might be expected and did not hesitate in recommending preparation to meet any emergency looking to hostility which might be brought about by this bad feeling. And it can plainly be seen that this late news spread a shadow of gloom over the whole region, and the happiness which was in the grasp of the people slipped out from their hands, and has never returned, even to this day.

When the war begun, it was brought on by the disappointed class, and it was carried on in such a scale it was not so destructive as it was feared, for instead of uniting, the leaders of the disappointed preferred to achieve heroic honors without the aid of their fellow disappointed spiritual brethren.   They would only select a few from their followers whom they led to battle.   Every spiritual man who lead the men to battle are called, "Mur-oo-wet,"—The commander.

The weapons used in the battle were the "Tur-bee" and "Par-queh," bow and arrow.   "Ed-dunk-he-gan," stone sling and the "Ms-squar-jees," war club.   And in time of war no mercy was shown to the defenseless, old people and women were despatched to eternity when found, even the little babes were slain, no prisoners of war taken, only such ones the enemy knows to be most beloved and esteemed, such persons are taken alive only to be cruely tortured; this is done to irritate the feelings of the prisoners friends.   Burning at the stake was the principal measure meted out to the unfortunate captives.   Exchange of prisoners was never entered into nor practiced.   The only way to rescue a friend from the enemy is to keep on fighting and if successful in routing the enemy, and if in his flight had not time to stop and slay the prisoners, your friend be restored to you alive.   The war was carried on mostly in the night time, the invading army watches closely and only when he finds the invaded to be in his sleep when the attacks are made.   The selected portion of the spiritual men never made practice only to be on the defense.   All of the battles were created and brought on by the disappointed, and the attacks were made by them.   Only twice did the selected spiritual men make an aggressive movement, which we will mention in another page.   In all this war period

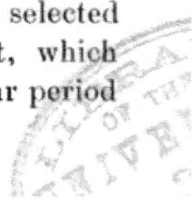

the spiritual men resorted to all sorts of spiritual power they possessed during the raging of the battle.

In some instances when closely cornered, would disappear on the spot, other times only some swift footed animal be seen leaving the battle ground, while others would turn into birds and fly away. Although the spiritual men had all been taught never to use the spiritual power in subduing the other by taking life, yet in times of war many cases of disregard to the teaching was shown, regardless of the pain of losing it, therefore some lively chase often took place, and in such a case, when a spiritual man chases another and has the power to overtake the other, that will be the end of the one overtaken, and in such a case the remains of the slain never was found because the slayer never tells what became of his victim nor how the conquest was accomplished. The object in all the wars was only to subdue one another. The conquerer never takes possession any part of the country that he conquers, nor require any indemnity from the conquered ; will not even take away things belonging to them, though in some instances some useful things were destroyed. There were very few battles fought in the day time ; such battles took place only when two opposite armies met by accident. According to the account given by the latest traditional story tellers, this foolish and cruel war was carried on many seven times seven years or until two certain young men had grown up among the selected class. These two were most wonderful being. They were a mystery to all, and were mysterous on account of their most wonderful power which they claimed to be spiritual.

They had the power that when in battle and in giving the war cry or yell, all the enemy that hears them, falls to the ground and lay helpless for a long time to the mercy of their enemy, and in this way and by these means the selected became victors in many of the minor battles. It so happened that there were no big battles took place while these two reigned in battles, because their power had become known among the disappointed and they were very shy of them. But of course the people of the land have increased so much and have covered such a vast portion of the country, they were not able to cover the whole of it with their protection, therefore the enemy had some chances in committing depredations and murders among some families living on the outskirts of the country, but this did not continue very long. Meeting repulses on every hand and knowing that they had created a bitter feeling among whom they considered their enemies, and realizing the danger awaiting them, sought safety and started southward in search of those that had gone before, who went away south when the ice laid on the land. The old men of the land did not advise them to stay, but on the contrary, were rather anxious to have them go. When the people knew this there was a great rejoicing because it was then thought that the trouble had passed away, and another selection was made from among the spirited men to aid those who had been so true and faithful in watching the movements of the people who had been seen sailing on the coast. In making the selection the two young men whose power was found to be so wonderful were

retained to guard the people against all invasion. A
name was given to each of those young men, and it
was the first time that any person received such a distinction so young as these young men were. The old
men gave one of them the name of "Menus-kose,"—
Ocean Island, and the other, "Mundo-ok-koke,"—Devil
slayer.

While these two men were young in age their power
was not needed as the enemy had gone so far south
that it was thought they would never return. Peace
did reign for a long while and during this intervale
those that were sent to follow and watch the movements of the strange people had returned and gave an
accurate account of their discoveries, the description of
those people, the size of their large canoe which was
propelled by a brown colored cloth spread in the wind,
and had smaller canoes lashed on the side of the large
one, which the hairy men would lower to the water,
get into them and move around in them every time the
big canoe finds a quiet and safe harbor in which it can
lay while the men be out examining the shores,
islands, coves and rivers. The men that were sent out
to watch these people made practice to secrete themselves from the view of these strange people until
their big canoe had sailed far out in the ocean and got
beyond their sight, which was done between sunset and
sunrise. Seeing that the big canoe had gone out of
sight, heading when last seen in the southern direction,
 then the watchmen directed their course toward their
homes, which they gladly reached after having been
absent for many moons and when they reached their

people they were gladly received by them. Previous to the return of the watchmen, some young men were out on a hunting expedition, who, when getting upon a high point of land overlooking the sea, beheld a large craft in plain view to them, moving very briskly before the strong wind then blowing, and the craft was heading south. These young men were so far away from their people, the strange craft had sailed out of sight before they could call their people's attention to it. The report of the young men of what they had seen was confirmed by the watchmen when they arrived home from their watching expedition. The stories of the two parties in giving their description of the big canoe agreed in every respect. All told how that the craft was going south. The story told by those that were sent to watch was to the effect, that they followed the people up into a large river which was so wide at its mouth that they did not cross its waters, because their canoes were so small they considered it a dangerous thing to undertake and were obliged to keep near the land on the south side of the river. But the strange people went up it so far the river became much narrower and their small canoe could cross it without much difficulty. And it was here that they made so close examination of the craft, especially in the night time when it was very dark, they were so close to it, they could easily hear the people talk in a language they could not understand.

These people must be great lovers of fish food as they could be seen fishing every calm morning. They would haul very large fishes up over the side of their

7

big canoe; and these people did not carry anything
away only some water. In those days a man of falsehood was not known among them therefore everything
these men told was fully believed, which established
the fact that white man had come to the red man's
world. This discovery was not looked upon as anything strange, since it has been foretold by the old
prophets; every body looked for it, even the children
expected it. Since the belief of the coming of the
white man had been so well established, there was
plenty of work for the old men! All the daily topics
was on this subject; meetings of the old men were frequently held, and the subject on what course to take
upon the matter was carefully and seriously considered,
and after the subject had been fully discussed by all the
people throughout the country, it was thought best, and
was so decided, that when the strange people came, to
receive them as friends, and if possible make brothers
of them.

After this sentiment had been planted in the hearts
and minds of all the people, all the attention was then
directed to the movements of the discontented who had
withdrawn, or whose act of secession was still so fresh
in the minds of the people. Seeing that they had
increased greatly in numbers during the many times
seven years of almost silent interval, had become bold
and had sought the way to carry out the vow they had
made and proclaimed upon their going out.

Frequent reports have come, how they have been
seen and threatening to do violence among the people
who are living in the extreme southern part of the

country, not only capturing some defenseless persons and torturing them, but in many cases carry off captives for the purpose of torture, and would, after carrying them far away from home leave them there either to die or find their way home the best they could, leaving no food for them.

The women captives liberated in this manner were allowed to go unbound, but the other sex was always securely bound so that they could not feed or otherwise help themselves; thus many suffered in that way.

Up to this period no lives had been taken outright; those suffered death met it by the results of the cruel tortures. When all this trouble being known, it spread like the wild fire and the excitement it caused was intense, the feeling it created so bitter it was almost beyond control especially when it was known as being the works of the spiritual men of the enemy. This bitter feeling was somewhat allayed by the advice of the old men who immediately called in all of their spiritual men whom they urged to begin an active operation against the enemy, not only to protect their people, but also to make a move to subdue the enemy's spiritual warriors. Thus the red man's war was declared and begun. In this war, if it be called such, the head ones of it were the spiritual men, and naturally it was conducted in a manner to their direction, therefore some very curious tactics were resorted to, and many puzzling aspects were witnessed by those who were not familiar with the spiritual power. In some of these engagements the leaders, or the spiritual men met first, because they are always at the head of their forces, very often without giving orders to their men, plunged headlong into battle between themselves, using all the power there was in them, while the rest of the forces be looking on. Here the none-spiritual often see some queer sights while waiting the results of the battle between their leaders. When in such engagements, the spiritual men show such a power that they were able to disappear in an instant and in a moment later reappear on a far different spot from where last seen, and when one conquers, would be seen coming toward their men which the conquered force is not slow in perceiving, because it is to them as a signal to make a hasty retreat for safety or fight without a leader, and when a retreat thus being made, it is then the conqueror pursues, kills or take such prisoners they wished. No one was ever known being saved and life spared by surrendering, therefore each one must struggle hard for an escape or to fight till disabled, or the death blow comes. In those days the power of the spiritual men were not alike, there were some who could see a long distance, and others can hear a long way, some can send their voices through the air to any distance desired, while others had the power in their war cry or yell that it takes away the strength of those they intend to disable so they fall to the ground and lay helpless for some moments and become an easy prey to the enemy.

This peculiar power was never known to exist among the warriors of the south, and it is due to this that the southern forces abandoned their aggressive expeditions northward for many years, and during this quiet period some explorers from the south came along east in their canoes. These explorers were old women who had paddled their canoe all the way along the coast from "Koeh-suk" at the pines, seeking to find the oyster and clam beds which the people found and lived on during their temporary stay while on their journey south after seceding from the north. Being women with old age, they were not molested but were allowed to do their errand. They were no other but the old women, yet they were very closely watched in all their movements and doings.

After exploring different points, these old women discovered the oyster beds and were able to locate the very spot. Not only oysters found at the place, but there were also forests of oak bearing acorns in the close proximity. When this was known the people rejoiced, and the old men were allowed to make a promise to the southern old women who had come and made this discovery, that they will be allowed to come and gather such supply as they wished for winter use so long as their people will not meddle the poor and infirm on either side during the harvesting for the winter supply, and if, after they have returned home to their people will call together seven of their old men, and will induce them to come north, they would not be molested, but an arrangement will be made with them so that the old and infirm both from the north and the south may have an equal privilege to come and get their winter supply of oysters and acorns unmolested. This generous offer of the old men of the north so pleased the old women of the south, it affected them very much and they made a solemn vow and promise that the offer

will be accepted, and that the old men of the south may
be looked for who will come to help make some wise
arrangements.

Very early the next season, the seven old men did
come, when a wholesome treaty was made, which
was always observed and well kept. These oyster
beds were so productive that it gave a supply to all
that wished for the period of many times seventy years,
so that the shells of this food fish was piled up almost
mountain high on the shore of a river bank for a long
distance. And the oyster period was enjoyed to within quite recently, so that the mounds of these shells
can now be plainly seen on the coast of Maine. Clam
beds were also found later, pretty near the spot of the
oyster beds, a little toward the direction of the rising
sun. All these shell fish were cured by drying.

Although the people stay around those oyster beds
or near them almost the year round, but those who lived
far away did not visit the place until just before the
leaves began to fall, they then go there and gather oysters, clams and acorns for winter use. The oysters
and clams were dried in the sun, and when they have
been sufficiently dried are packed in "Mik-nur-queh—
birch bark packing box," in which they can be kept
until winter. The "Ar-nass-cum-nal"—acorns, were
also gathered in their season and dried ; and in the
winter time, a family wishing to have a fashionable
dinner, cooks the dried oysters in water, well seasoned
with the bear or seal oil, and after the oysters are well
soaked and boiled, the pounded acorns were added
enough to give it a good flavor. The clams were

secured, cooked and served precisely the same way. As has been stated before, that this place was set apart and reserved for all the old and infirm ; therefore when the harvest time comes the place contained many people from all parts of the country, and here they exchanged a great deal of information, and in this way the people of the north learned all about the southern people. Those that came from the south, seeing that they had the same privileges in common with the northern people, felt very friendly and did not hesitate in giving a full account of their people at the south, and through these exchanges it was learned that while on their voyage south, and when these oyster beds were discovered, some wanted to go back home, or place where their home had been, and join their people and friends again in peace, but their leaders, the spiritual men opposed to any and all such propositions and urged the people on further south. And after a long time, a dispute arose among the non-spiritual, which in time resulted in dividing the people again. Having already made a good selection of the country and had been located, many concluded to make this land to be their home, while others preferred to take backward steps toward the north, because they were very much disheartened in learning they were to fight for their existence.

The supply of the stone to make the arrow heads and spear becoming scarce with them, a party of men were sent south to explore the region for the purpose of finding such stone. These men after travelling seven summers and winters, crossing many large rivers

and lakes, and after seeing another ocean extending
towards the setting sun, did find some such a stone,
but none could be found on the shores same as in the
north; what they found was on the base of the mountains away from any sea shore, and brought home so
small an amount of it, did not give such encourage-
ment as was expected. The spiritual men could hold
the people together no longer and were obliged to let
such portion go that wished; a large part of them
came toward the north, only a small number going
further south, and just how far south was never defin-
itely known. Some of them, comprising the largest part
concluded to remain on the spot previously selected,
because it was near the mouth of a river abounding with
game and fish; oysters were also found but the beds of
them were small and produced but a little, more clams
and seal were found than oysters, and for this, the portion
that were dissatisfied came north and located on the southern shore of a large bay where clams, seal and eels
were found in abundance, and after making a settlement on the place the name given to it was "Go-eh-suk"
—at the pines. This name was given to it because
every point of land in the bay was covered with the
growth of pine, hence the name of "Go-eh-suk."
From this place the old women who have been already
mentioned, started toward the north to hunt up the
oyster beds which they found as has been stated before.
The people of the north hearing these reports, caused
them to be contented; and after this wholesome arrangement had been entered into, the visits of the southern
men for the purpose of committing depredation ceased

for a long period, which brought much happiness. But this did not last always, as after many years the southern old people brought a report, that the people at Go-eh-suk, was about to be led by a War-Spirited man who has assumed the name of "War-har-weh,— greatest of all," who has declared a revenge against the north, was bound to enter into mischief making and was coming north. The whole northern country having enjoyed peace so long, and the spiritual power had been waning and passing away to nothing, this news caused a great alarm, as none were known to possess the power the men had who were then dead and gone, Munus-kose and Mundo-ark-koke had both died with the old age, and none were known to have filled their places, the people did not feel secure. However the preparations were made to meet any emergency with such power they then had. It was not long when War-har-weh made his appearance at the extreme southern part of the north, made an attack on the inhabitants, killing many, took and carried away many prisoners. When this was done, the whole north was aroused to a high pitch, runners were sent out to carry and spread the news, and a general assembly of the country was called which was readily responded to by the whole north, and a war was declared against Go-eh-suk, and to subdue War-har-weh. In about seven moons, a large fleet of canoes were seen sailing on the coast heading for Go-eh-suk. The point of land where War-har-weh had located his headquarters had been so minutely given by the old people from that section, the northern forces knew exactly where to go and when to make the attack.

All the arrangements were so well made and plans laid that when the place was reached in the night time, the advanced scouts had no difficulty in arranging for a successful attack. The scouts discovered War-har-weh's headquarters on a high hill overlooking the sea, as well as the bays, which could be reached from the main land by a sand bar or peninsular which extended to the hill where War-har-weh was supposed to be sleeping. This sand bar was covered with the growth of sand grass, therefore it was called "Nan-sus-kek," grassy fore-ground. The location of War-har-weh's wigwam had been so clearly described by the old people it was easily found and attacked. But the darkness of the night was in War-har-weh's favor, and he was able to give them the slip and got away unhurt by hiding himself among the eel grass near the water on the bay side of the sand bar where he laid till near morning, when he emerged from his hiding place and walked out on the eel grass flats and swam across a small river just before the break of day, got into a thick forest, leaving his people to the mercy of the enemy. When the northern men found that the inhabitants were not so many as had been expected, did not enter into slaughtering the women and children, but took a good care in killing the men, saving only such prisoners they could easily carry away with their own people who had been brought there captives by War-har-weh. Many prisoners were killed after daylight before the eyes of the women and children. War-har-weh's wife was among them, and when asked who she was, bravely said that she was the wife of War-har-weh, and also pointed out her only son who was among the captives. This young man's life was spared and he was securely bound and was carried north with the other prisoners. Knowing that they had secured War-har-weh's son, and that he would go north after him after things had quieted, the army did not tarry long on the ground, was soon embarked in the canoes and was soon heading for "Qua-nee-bek," Long Blade, at the north; and when the mouth of Qua-nee-bek was reached, here the prisoners were landed and taken to a high bluff of land, and a large force was placed there to guard them, because it was thought that War-har-weh would not make much delay in coming after his son. Before the big army was temporarily disbanded, a large meeting was held, and in this meeting an agreement and plan was made to the effect, that when War-har-weh came, no matter whether he be for peace or war, he shall be beheaded and all that comes with him.

As had been predicted, it was not long when a canoe was seen on the coast coming north, containing only three persons. The number being so small, was allowed to approach unmolested which soon landed where many was standing to receive them. Seeing this and upon being approached, the head of the three stepped forth holding up the pipe of peace, signifying what they had come for, were soon conducted to a wigwam which had been vacated for the purpose, and into this wigwam they were allowed to enter, and a strong guard was put upon it. Here War-har-weh made known his mission. The answer given him was, that in seven suns an answer will be given him. Runners were immediately sent out, calling in all that can come

within the time specified.   And this call brought out
about all the North to witness the execution.   The
number that came was so great that the land was
literally covered with people ; And as there being no
wigwam large enough to hold this vast assemblage, an
open spot of land was selected where the council was
held.   When meeting had been called to order, the first
move War-har-weh made was to produce the pipe of
peace which he handed over to his friend who was
seated next to him and commanded him to rise and hold
the pipe up high, while War-hah-weh turned and immediately
began to unpack his pack, and after this was done he
began to plead and asked for   peace.   Showing a large
amount of wampun and other valuables which he had
brought and wished to give as a ransom for his son's release.
Immediately after War-har-weh had ended his talk, "Nequ-
tar-tar-wet"—The Lone Star, who was then the greatest war
leader of the north stepped in front and told War-har-weh
that his doom had already been sealed, and it was his duty
to tell him that as he never had shown peace nor mercy to
the women and children, his and his friends heads shall be
taken off their bodies.   And Nequ-tar-tar-wet here gave the
signal to the three men who had been placed close in the rear
of the doomed men, who, upon seeing the signal immediately
grasped the long hair of each of the men whose heads are to
be taken off, and with a well directed aim with their long war
knives, two heads were held up to Nequ-tar-tar-wet, but
the third man missed his stroke and the southern man
managed to break away by getting on his feet and gaining an

open space after passing through the vast crowd, ran
for dear life. But unfortunately for the poor man, a flank
guard had previously been placed so that in case an escape
was made, none of those escaped could reach the main land.
The man saw this and turned to a space that he saw laid
open for him, although this open space led to the highest
bluff of the land, a precipice of rock, yet, to this he ran ; some
swift footed young warriors ran in pursuit, but the man
gained the bluff. Seeing he could run no further nor retreat
back, kept on, and when the edge of the precipice was
reached, he made a high leap off the precipice saying as he
leaped, "Ar-gur-muk," meaning "over to the other land,"
but the poor fellow did not reach there but was dashed to
pieces among the rocks below.

Thus ended all War-har-weh's mission. When quiet had
been restored and war assembly was about to be dissolved,
it was decreed that the heads of the two warriors be pre-
served and shall be taken through the northern and eastern
countries, from place to place by seven women. This exhibi-
tion was intended to show what will be the fate whoever
undertakes to disturb the peace of the north as War-har-weh
had done. This order of the assembly was strictly carried
out, these heads were exhibited from place to place for seven
years. There still remained four prisoners in the hands of the
northern people, who had been captured and brought north
by the army that subdued War-har-weh ; these were all
young men, and War-har-weh's son was among them. They
all had been forced to witness the execution of
their warriors. These young men had not been cruelly

tortured as might have been expected, but were closely guarded and watched, having shown no desire to escape were allowed many privileges, and the treatment extended to them was as good as can be expected under like circumstances. Without doubt, these young men must have laid plans for their escape while receiving so good a treatment, because not many years had elapsed when one fine morning the young War-har-weh was missing, which led to an investigation concerning the other three, and the result of the investigation revealed that the other three prisoners were missing, and two nice canoes and a good outfit of paddles could not be found. These two canoes were never seen afterward. This escape was considered to be so small a matter no pursuit was made, therefore these young men safely reached Go-eh-suk, which they found deserted, and upon going further south they found some of their own folks among those that were living there.

When these were forced to flee for safety from the clutches of the northern army, many of the young warriors kept on further south in search of the ones who had gone that way, and who had been known to ascend a large river, which bore its direction toward the north land, which was named, "Watch-we-took"—River of mountains.

CHAPTER VI.

The winding up the war with the May-Quays.—The grand council established—The arrival and settlement of the white man.

THESE people having gone so far away, the northern
people never followed them, therefore never penetrated
that part of the country and knew very little about it.
This much however was known, that after many years
these scattered people came together and located themselves on the west shore of the big river and called
themselves the "May-Quay," May-May people, and after
many years were known as the Mohawks.

This scattered portion of the red people being all
young and strong they naturally had the inclination of
becoming warlike, but being afraid of the northern
power did not venture to molest that country. They
learned this from some minor raids they tried to carry
out, which in all of them, met with ready-handed squads
to repulse them. They were obliged to adopt the kid-
napping game, and would steal persons and carry them
off as prisoners, and having met with some success in
this, became more bold, and began to kill more freely.
When this kind of work begun, the whole north took
it into its hand to subdue and do away with the whole
thing. When this was undertaken, the work was so
planned and executed that the May-Quay's hope of
mastery was forever blasted in a manner as will be
mentioned later.

When War-har-weh's son and the other prisoners made their escape there was no attempt made to pursue them, the principal reason was of this, that just at this time an exciting news was brought from the extreme north to the effect, that the white man's big canoe had come again, and had landed its people who are still remaining on the land on the north shore of the "Ma-quozz-bem-to-cook, Lake River," and have planted some heavy blocks of wood in the form of a cross. These people are white and the lower part of the faces of the elder ones are covered with hair, and the hair is in differ-ent colors, and the eyes are not alike, some have dark while others have light colored eyes, some have eyes the color of the blue sky. They have shown nothing only friendship, they take the red man's hands in their own and bow their heads down and make many signs in the direction of the stars ; and their big canoe is filled with food which they eat and also give some to those that come to them and made signs of friendship. When this news spread, the people took it so quietly and talked about it in such a way, there was no excitement, but everybody took it as though it was an old affair, yet it had such effect upon them, that it was evident that the general desire was, that the habits of the strange people must be well learned, and all agree to wait and see what kind of a treatment they will extend to the red people. If the treatment they have already extended be continued, it was thought will be the means of bringing happiness to both races. This was the conclu-sion reached, which after many years proved to be so wise, because it was upon this conclusion strictly lived up to, that the red man of the north never had any trouble with the white man.

Although the white man has given his hand as a brother, yet, the distrust on the part of the red man was great, which had been led to it by the action and bad conduct of the May-Quays. Anticipating trouble from all quarters, knowing not from whence, or how it will come, the happiness of the north, as might be expected soon became almost "The thing of past." Here, on one side a strange people have begun to plant themselves almost in their midst, while on the other, their own people making raids upon their weakest points; still the attention they were bound to give to this strange white man never for a moment wavered, because the stranger's action toward them was of such a nature and so impressive, no hostilities toward him was talked, nor even thought of.

The signs of brotherhood has been manifested by him so plainly that everyone having the chance of meeting him, greets him with the "Nitchieh,"—brother. Because all his actions were taken as such. But the most striking character of his works was in his endeavors in converting the people to become believers in his spiritual teachings ; being yet a whole believer in the spiritual power, the red man, when taught thus, readily conceived the idea and believed in such teaching and was ready to wait and see the outcome of it.

Meanwhile the works of those terrible May-Quay's had become so unbearable that something must be done to quell it, even if they had to be wiped out of the land forever, because many people have already been

8

converted and were not only believers, but followers of
the white man's doctrine and it had made such a
change in them they knew enough to be cautious and
slow in their movements in this direction. Seven years
was agreed upon to make a general aggressive move.
And during these seven years of council a well
planned campaign had been perfected. Although the
people had already been well scattered to the South,
North, East and West, yet by careful canvassing it was
found that all were having the same mind ; and it was
also found among those that emigrated to other parts
of the country, had received the doctrine of the white
man and all wanted peace. To make a permanent affair
of it, an act of federation was adopted by all the
north, embracing the north of "Ko-chi-koke,"—a great
gum river, extending to the extreme east of "Mik-
murk-keag,"—the youngest land, and as far west as
"Odur-wur-keag,"—father land. Seven years was
found a sufficient time in which to make all necessary
arrangements and a war cry was to be heard all over the
land, and an outbreak of the May-Quays was anxiously
looked for at the same time. Whether through
a spy or otherwise, they must have known what
was up, because they did not venture out on any
raiding expedition for at least another seven
years. And during all these years, they were closely
watched and were at last discovered to be on
the move with a large force, heading for Mik-mur-keag;
and the route selected was down the Ma-qozz-bem-to-
cook. They had scarcely made the move when a war
signal was given all over the land ; Odur-wer, came
down on the same river not far in May-Quay's rear ;

others rushed from their quarters and in a very few days all of the northern forces met at the extreme eastern part of Mik-mur-keag ; but not a trace of May-Quays had been discovered by the parties that came from all directions, yet they were, when last seen, coming down the river in canoes; Odur-wur, who also came down the same river in canoes saw nothing of them. After the army had got together the leaders of it met in council and it was decided to hunt them up and to wind up the war with them if possible. A careful search was being made on both sides of the big river and all the small branches carefully examined, but no trace of them could be found. A sand Island, near the mouth of "Tur-too-saqu,"—ledge door, was passed several times, but being a baren sand Island and could be examined with the eye from the distant waters, it was not expected that they would be on it, in fear of being easily found, therefore the army passed by it several times, yet the May-quays were on that Island, buried in the sand, not only themselves but their canoes were buried as well so that not a vestige could anyone have seen unless he was stepping on them, and in this way they escaped detection. And when the search was being abandoned in that part of the river, a canoe was seen coming down containing four men, who were allowed to approach and were found to be friends, and had come to join them in their war. These folks reported that they had made a very close observations of all parts of the country and had discovered nothing of the enemy, a change of tacties was then adopted, because it was then supposed that the enemy was on the sand Island ; so a stratagem was planned and put into operation in this manner; that the same canoe that came down, after taking out two of its passengers and the remaining two to go along toward the mouth of Tur-too-saqu, on a hunting pretense. They are to be looking for game from place to place until the mouth of the river reached, then if no signs of the enemy being discovered, they are to strike out with all possible haste directly for the sand Island and when they have reached the latter place, when nearing its shore to sing out "Quai" a well known salute among hunters when they meet. Being thus saluted they will naturally feel that have been discovered, and will strive hard to capture or kill their discoverers so as to be able to further elude the pursuing party if there was one on their track.

As a lively chase was expected to follow, the route of retreat laid out was to be directly back to the mouth of Tur-too-saqu, and if closely pursued run up it, until a good landing place is reached, and if still pursued run ashore, leave the canoe and run up the moutain, take a circuitous route to the shore of the big river where there will be a small squad detailed to pick them up; and if not successful in the first attempt in drawing out the enemy, make another effort after resting half day. This second attempt will surely draw them out, because they then will be fully convinced that they have been discovered; and if the second attempt drew out nothing, to come to the main force when some other plan be tried. The second attempt, however, was not needed, because when these hunters got within a hailing distance of the island, saw a man on the move from one place to another, and to this man the hunters shouted "Quai,"

who responded with a signal yell which brought the
whole army out of the sand where it had been laying hid
for several days. Without making further examination,
the hunters turned the bow of their canoe shoreward
and pulled for Tur-too-saqu, while the enemy clambered,
and lifted their canoes out of the sand mounds, launched
and filled them with warriors and gave a chase. Those
that were launched on the side of the island next to
the fugitives got on the chase so much sooner, they got
far in advance before the rest of the force got under-
way on the chase; meanwhile the northern army which
had been silently drifting down by the island during
the previous night, and had disembarked and had hidden
their canoes in the bushes, rushed out with them and
and was soon on the scene of this grand chase. The
enemy seeing this and perceiving the magnitude of its
army, immediately began to show signs of bewilder-
ment, and in their perplexity attempted to recall, and
even pulled to head off the rest of their force from
further pursuit; but that part of the force got so far
in advance, knew nothing of what was taking place
behind them kept on chasing the hunters. About one-
third of the May-Quay's army was in this hot pursuit
while the balance of it whirled and began to pull back
for the sand Island. But this was useless, as the
northerners had anticipated this, and had laid plans to
avert it, and without much effort headed off the May-
Quay army which they soon surrounded and disarmed
mid the waters of the Great Lake river. Both armies
then rested and looked on to see the two squads who
are both on a chase. The May-Quay's did not know

that they were being pursued until just before reaching
the mouth of Tur-too-saqu, then only when their pursuers got so near upon them that they heard the racket
made by them, when the leader of the May-Quays
looked around and saw that they were being closely
pursued by the enemy, and who had already got the
space between him and his friends, undertook to turn
and slip by his pursuer and get back to the main force;
but the quick-eyed northerner would not allow this
done when he could so easily prevent it by making a
flank move which he did, which caused the May-
Quays to turn again and continue on towards Tur-too-
saqu which they soon reached, and ran along near the
shore, and when an opportunity offered, jumped out of
their canoes, ran up the mountain while their pursuers
were close at their heels. In this way the two squads
flew up the mountain, and when May-Quay saw the
hopelessness of making further effort to escape, made
a stand from which to give a battle. This battle was a
fierce one which lasted all the rest of the day. And
when night was fast approaching with no apparent gain
on either side, the leaders on both sides being great
warriors got very much excited over the day's work,
both got exasperated over its outlook, both at the same
moment determined to bring the matters to a close by
making one great and the last effort, decided to use the
spiritual power that was in them, which both had been
hesitating to bring to bear upon their fellowmen;
knowing that when they use it in that way, it will
depart from them forever, therefore hesitated to resort
to such work. But things had got so far that discretion

was no longer a part of valour, both at the same
moment, unbeknown to each, stepped in front, gave
the earth a violent stamp with the right foot, at the
same time throwing his war weapons savagely on the
earth. This was done to start an earthquake, and it
so happened in this case that the leaders of both of
these forces possessed the same power, and by apply-
ing it at the same moment caused a severe earthquake
to follow, and so severe was it, it not only shook things,
but the earth itself parted and swallowed up both
forces while they were thus engaged in a deadly conflict;
leaving only the two leaders on both sides standing, and
listening to the screeches made by the men they had
been leading; screeches issuing from under the earth
where these poor men are forever shut up. Seeing
what they had done, and knowing that by using and
abusing the spiritual power in the manner they did, was
a sufficient cause for them to lose the art, so they both
advanced to each other, shook hands, and made peace
over the chasm. And while on their way back to their
people, made the compromise that they shall both abide
by the results of the works of their main forces to
which they belonged. The main forces were not idle
while all this was going on up in the mountains.
Everything had been all settled on the water where the
May-Quays were held prisoners, and the two forces
were waiting to get the news from their respective
squads and hear the results. When night was nearing,
the old warriors said that there must be a hard battle
raging between the two squads somewhere up the Tur-
too-saqu. At this, the May-Quays showed signs of

uneasiness, while the northerners had so much confidence in their men waited with all possible quietude and calmness. This drifting around in the river was kept up all night, and when the morning came, when the sun was just rising, a canoe was seen coming directly toward the armies, and when the canoe arrived it was found to contain the two leaders of the squads who had been chasing one another for the last day and night. It did not take long for the returned leaders to relate and make known what had been taking place up among the mountains and what had become of their friends. When the May-Quays knew this it agitated their spirit very much and finally asked to be allowed to withdraw from where they were then kept to consult among themselves so that they may come to a final conclusion what action to take to settle their situation, and no doubt but that they may enter into what may be expected of them in the future. A short consultation was allowed them, and they were allowed to withdraw from their captors, who took such a precaution that they took all the paddles from their captives leaving them floating about without them, and were only allowed to keep together by holding their canoes while the consultation was being held. The northerners having withdrawn to a short distance from them also held a consultation to see what to do with the prisoners. It did not take long for them to decide that should the prisoners ask for anything other than a permanent peace, all the best warriors shall be slain leaving only a few to escape death who shall receive a permanent mark upon their person, such as cutting off the ears, nose, or an eye plucked out, after which be allowed to go their way in peace. While this council was holding, the May-Quay gave the signal that their conference had ended, and the northerners immediately repaired to join them. Upon getting together, the May-Quays made a vow with great solemness, that if allowed, they would live in peace with all the people in all times to come, and were ready then to accede to any and all things required of them. The northerners, though conquerors, yet upon hearing such declaration gave them great joy, and another council was immediately held, and in this, the prayer of the prisoners was granted. And in order to satisfy all who had been troubled more or less with the past wars, a place was selected where a grand council fire was to be located and established, where all the heads of clans which had previously been changed into tribes, shall go once in seven years to renew the council fire and talk over matters for the general good. And it was here decreed that the prisoners shall establish their quarters on the place designated, there to take care of the council fire, and whenever a delegation comes to the grand council fire to renew it, they shall furnish food for all that come and shall furnish shelter and give all necessary comfort during the stay of the delegation without pay. This was the proposition submitted to May-Quays which they readily accepted, and a treaty of this nature was made, and to make it lasting, a large collection of wampum was made from all parts of the country which was afterwards woven into a wampum band two hands wide and twenty-one hands long, and along in the middle part many different characters were woven in, representing what the band was made for and who are concerned in it. This band was the grand council fire which was left in the care of the May-Quays who were very faithful to their duty until very recently when they began to show signs of change in their demenour which was soon discovered, and the visits to the grand council fire was after a while stopped. This discontinuance was brought about by the action of Odur-wur which was soon followed by all the other tribes.

The spot selected where the grand council fire was to be established was at the head of the first big rapids of the great lake river, and the name given to it was "K'chi-skoo-tek," grand council fire. As has been stated before, that all the tribes visit this council fire every seven years, and during the council days all kinds of sports were enjoyed by the young class.

At first the May-Quays seemed pleased to have the people come, and took much pride in being able to entertain decently all that came, and always seemed delighted in serving as the keeper, but after a long while wanted to be the commander, wanted to be boss, this the people could not tolerate, and quit going there. The last visit made from the east was only fifty-three years ago, and some of the young men that went with the old men on that last visit are still living. One feature of the federation that can be called pleasant, is that the people divided themselves into three classes, the father, eldest son and the youngest son. "Odur-wur" was the father, "Wur-bar-Nar-ki,—dawn lander," the eldest son, and "Mik-Mur,—the last born" was the

youngest son. And after the division was made
the oldest Mik-mur present, was undressed and put
into "T'ki-nur-gann",—cradle, where he was kept tied
and fed all day like the little babe, and every time the
delegation met at the grand council fire this perform-
ance was repeated, which shows that the Mik-mur was
once selected as the youngest of all, he must always be
treated like a little baby. And again, what made
the other part of this treaty more harmonizing and
solemn, and has carried its impression into the minds
of all the generations that followed was, that after the
May-Quays made their final surrender to the northerners, the two young warriors who escaped the earthquake were made to lead both of the armies to the
spot where the two squads had been sunk, and upon
reaching the place which had been the battle ground, all
was found in much confusion, nothing but the signs of the
late eruption of the earth could be seen. But the
screeches of the poor creatures that were shut up under
the earth could be plainly heard. So plainly were they,
that the words they uttered could be understood by those
that listened. Their cry is for peace, and nothing but
peace. These screeches were so pitiful and susceptible
they caused much feeling among all that heard them, the
strongest and the hardest heart could resist no longer,
but every heart melted and joined in the agreement that
this spot shall always be held sacred in the hearts of all
the people, and that the peace made over its chasm shall
stand forever, and the people shall visit the sacred spot
at least once in seven years. This agreement was
well observed and kept up by all the people and the

spot was visited quite frequently for many times seventy
years, and every time the ground being visited the
screeches of these poor creatures who are shut up there
can be heard very plain.

This ended all the wars among the red people.
Next follows the coming of the white man, as has been
stated, the strange people had already planted blocks
of wood in the form of a cross, and also how kind and
brotherly he was, had such a weight in the heart of the
red man the people waited with much interest to see
him come again.   The conquest of the northerners over
the May-Quays was so pleasing to all the people they
were ready to accept anything offered them by almost
anyone in the form of peace, so when the white man
came and lived among them they were ready to receive
and believe his doctorine.   The reason of this ready
belief was because the teaching was similar to the one
the spiritual men of the people had been teaching, so
when the white man's missionaries came they had an
easy task in converting to its folds many and all that
could be reached.

At about this period another white man came in his
big canoe and landed on the shore of the eastern coast
almost in the midst of the northern country, on a high
island very near the spot where Klose-kur-beh and the
dog killed the first moose.   Here the white man planted
his cross, and here he lingered until after many other
white men came.   Here the red man received the
religion of the white man.   The red man was now
ready to be converted and resigned himself to wait for
the future fate that may come.

CONCLUSION.

NOT wishing to indulge too freely in the habit of negligence thereby leaving my readers in the dark on the very matters that the people wish, or ought to know, I deem it expedient, before coming to the final close with this work, to give the fullest account possible, of the daily life and convenience of these people who are now on the descending slide scale to a point not yet settled. First, I call the attention of the reader to the time when the red man looked upon, or was wholly dependent on the Great Spirit in furnishing him so to meet all his daily needs. But it was not long before he discovered that something must be done by man, especially in the matter of keeping the fire going, so that he could have it by him and set up a blaze when he wished, because there had been many instances where people were obliged to go without it for a long time. True, the Great Spirit would not let them suffer, and the idea of the people being in the same way, would diligently seek deliverance, and often scouring the country to find a small speck of fire from which they could gather their supply. There never was a time that they were obliged to return empty handed, but always found that being patient in the continuous hunt would find a tree that had been struck by lightning that still retained the fire that had been brought upon it. But the difficulty was how to keep

it burning while it was being transported from
one place to another, especially in the case where the
places are far apart.　Experiment solved that the outer
bark of the "Kunks-koosi,"—cedar tree, after having
been rubbed fine would take fire readily and keep
burning until it was all consumed; but on account of
its heavy smoke it would have to be carried in the hand
uncovered; yet, no other method was found that would
answer any better until after many years had elapsed
when it was discovered that some parts of the green
hard wood tree produced a dry, rotten wood now called
spunk, which substance would burn very slowly and
never go out until every speck of it had been consumed.
It burnt so slow that a very small piece lasted half a
day and emitted scarcely any smoke, so that it could
be carried in a pouch made for the purpose.　Then
came the question how to prepare it so it will not burn
the pouch.　Clam shells were found just what was
needed after having been lined with the blue clay and
a small aperture having been left open between the two
shells through which, what smoke there was might
escape; these shells were put together and tied
tightly and put into the pouch made of a whole skin of
the "Mo-nim-queh-so,"—woodchuck, which can be
carried on one's belt outside of all the garments.　No
part of the skin was sewed, having been skinned whole,
only one hole cut lengthwise from the base of the skull
down on the back long enough to admit the hand.　In
preparing the skin the skull after having the flesh well
scraped off and the bone dried, turned back into its
place, is then ready to be hung on the belt where it
will not slip out.

The tree that produces the best "Chi-quoqu-soqu,"—spunk, is the "Wee-quesk,"—yellow birch, and the shells used were not of the common "Aiss,"—clam, but it was the "Chim-quor-hur," which was of the thick and round species commonly know as the quahog. Being lined with the "Mur-sar-loon-esqu,"—blue clay, kept the heat in the shells sufficiently, and will not burn things so that the hunter and others were able to carry fire with them all the time.

After many years it was found necessary that something else must be found so that in case of all the fires be out that a fire might be brought when it was wanted without hunting for it. After much careful study, one young genius discovered that by having a speed wheel made from the inner bark of the yellow birch in three or four thicknesses, fastened together so that it will have some weight, and a small soft wood spindle two or three hands long, put through this wheel so that when the wheel whirls it would turn the spindle. The spindle must be longer from the wheel up than below it. To the top end of this spindle some fine strips of the skin of the "Na-hur-mo,"—eel, are fastened, allowing the strips to be in sufficient lengths so that when the wheel turns it carries the spindle with it and the strings would wind around the spindle, the other end of the strings being tied to another stick which is placed in a horizontal position with one of these strings on each end, and the spindle being in upright position so when the wheel is in motion it winds up the strings and the horizontal stick. When the operator finds the stick is well up to the top of the spindle, presses the stick down, it stops the whirl of the wheel and soon begins to revolve the other way, this repeated lively a blaze is brought at the foot of the spindle, a spunk is applied and a fire is had. This horizontal stick does not only act to turn the wheel but it also helps to hold up the whole machine. The foot part of the spindle where the fire is expected to come must be very dry, and the thing that turns on must be equally so.

The pouch in which the fire is carried was called "Pitson-ungun." To make a vessel to boil water was an easy thing to invent. It was simply to turn up the edges of the "Mus-queh,"—birch bark, so it will form a hollow part, and a small stick is bent and fastened around the top to hold the edges together. It is then ready to be filled with the "Neppi,"—water, and put on the "Skoo-teh,"—fire. This fire must be composed chiefly of hot coals, because if a blaze be allowed to run up to the top of the kettle it would soon burn off the fastenings.

"Sur-lur-waia,"—salt, was never used. "Sunk-kur-dee,"—needle, was a piece of bone found in certain parts of "Par-nar-kusso,"—sable. The little bone has an eye like the needle of to-day, and after sharpening the other end the needle is ready for use. But in sewing, the holes are first made with the "Magoos,"—awl, made from the tail of "So-paqui-tol-peh,"—sea turtle, which is of the horseshoe species. Dried common thorns,—"Kur-weesiark," were used as common pins. "Emquann,"—spoon, and "Quartsis,"—drinking cup, were both made of birch bark. In some instances the spoon is made of "Arparsi,"—wood. It is then called "Arpars-emquen." "Wur-bur-bee,"—wampum, is made from the different colored sea shells which are now extinct. The parts of the shell got out fit for use are rubbed on some gritty stone to shape them. Then the awl is used to make the holes. The making of the holes was the slowest part of the work, therefore when it was made it was considered valuable. It was never intended to be used as money. True there were many instances where it was exchanged for some other things, yet the principal object was that it only be used as the pledge of honor; say for instance, that whenever a person or persons wished their words to be taken honorably and give wampum with their words, will be sufficient to settle the thing desired. Matches for marriages were made by the old people and here the wampum is used as the pledge of honor on the man's part. Marriages are made by the young couple making a solemn vow and seven bows in silence toward the sun when it was highest on that day in presence of the old folks that made the match, who pronounced them "Nis-we Chik,"—husband and wife, after which the man follows his new bride to her folks where they are to stay two years at least.

Some names of the different places which have been mentioned in this work are found to have been corrupted by the white man in trying to speak the original words as were given by the red man. We find that the word "Goeh-suk,"—at the pines, has been changed to Cohasset, and then the word "Nan-sus-keg,"— grassy foreground, has been changed to Nantasket, also the word "Quen-ne-bek,"—long blade, to Kennebec.

And the word "Ar-gur-muk,"—over to the other land, has been changed to Hock Mock. The last mentioned place was where War-har-weh and his friend were beheaded, which is at the mouth of the Kennebec river. The name of "Mar-dar-mes-kun-teag,"—young shad pool has also been changed to Damariscotta. The country where so many oak acorns were harvested and where the oyster shell mounds can now be seen. The acorns are called "Ar-nas-com-nal,"—oak tree, "Ar-nas-com-messi," and oysters, "Mardes-sus-suk."

Reading and writing were never taught, the people had no notion of getting in that way until after they had divided themselves into clans. In forming and organizing the clans, some noted man is set up as the head of the clan, and the lineage of him is traced down to all the descendants who are claimed as the members of the clan.

Some took so much pride in their clans that they began to draw lines of distinction and adopted some animal, fish or fowl as the symbol of their class. This new idea set them up to writing or making marks, so that they could be understood by those who see them. Whenever a person enters into some new country, and wishes others to know that he had been there, makes a mark on the side of a tree where the bark had been knocked off, here the emblem of the clan is prominently pictured out.

Picture of a wigwam represents the home of the family; picture of a person facing from it means going from home; facing to it represents going home; picture of the Sun means day; the Moon, Month.

When a person writes the number of days of his absence, marks out the sun, and under it puts as many notches as there are days of his absence, and if it be months, uses the moon instead but exactly in the same manner. We will now mention one of each of the animals, fish and fowl that were adopted as the symbols for some clans. "Ar-wa-soose,"—bear, "Ar-na-tar-so,"—humming bird, and the fish sturgeon, "Kar-par-seh."

Besides the medicine prepared by the old women to heal the sick, there was found after many years, or just previous to the coming of the white man, a natural medicinal water in the vicinity of "Kars-koke,"—at the crane, which was found to contain very powerful healing powers, the effects which was very much the same as the medicine prepared by the healers, therefore it was considered very valuable, and the spot was visited by all the people from all parts of the country, and they continued their visits until after the white man came. The people did not wish to quit, nor go without enjoying the great benefit of this medicine water, and kept going there until the white man took possession of it. Since that time we have been informed that it has gone into the hands of an individual, a white man, of the town of Deering, Maine. According to the old traditional story tellers, this water boils out of the earth in a country of rocks a short walk from the shore of Kars-koke in the direction of the setting sun. This great medicine water was called "K'chit-ka-bi."

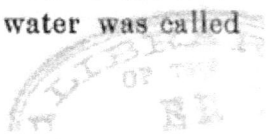

THE END.

www.ingramcontent.com/pod-product-compliance
Lightning Source LLC
Chambersburg PA
CBHW030600270326
41927CB00007B/989